77 Amazin
with (
Black & White Student Edition

© 2014 Califa Media®

WRITTEN BY

GRAND SHEIK BROTHER KUDJO ADWO EL
MOORISH SCIENCE TEMPLE OF AMERICA
SUBORDINATE TEMPLE #5 - TORONTO
CANAANLAND

GRAND SHEIK RAMI A. SALAAM EL
INTERNATIONAL ASIATIC MOORISH
HIP HOP TEMPLE
OAKLAND, CALIFORNIA,

EDITED BY
SHEIKESS TAUHEEDAH S. NAJEE-ULLAH EL
MOORISH SCIENCE TEMPLE CALIFORNIA, INC.
MOORISH SCIENCE TEMPLE CALIFA
RIVERDALE, ILLINOIS

Ibrahim A. Jalloh

77 Amazing Facts about Moors with Complete Proof
Black & White Student Edition

© 2014
Califa Media ®
RIVERDALE, ILLINOIS

WRITTEN BY
GRAND SHEIK KUDJO ADWO EL
MOORISH SCIENCE TEMPLE OF AMERICA
SUBORDINATE TEMPLE #5 - TORONTO
CANAANLAND

WRITTEN BY
GRAND SHEIK RAMI A. SALAAM EL
INTERNATIONAL ASIATIC MOORISH HIP HOP TEMPLE
OAKLAND, CALIFORNIA

EDITED BY
Sheikess Tauheedah S. Najee-Ullah El
MOORISH SCIENCE TEMPLE CALIFORNIA, INC.
MOORISH SCIENCE TEMPLE CALIFA

LIBRARY OF CONGRESS CONTROL NUMBER: 2015934769
ISBN-13: 978-1508629351
ISBN-10: 1508629358

All Rights Reserved. Without Prejudice. No Part Of This Book May Be Reproduced Or Transmitted In Any Form By Any Means, Electronic, Photocopying, Mechanical, Recording, Information Storage Or Retrieval System Unless For The Liberation Of Minds And Gaining Knowledge Of Self.

Califa Media
A Moorish Guide Publishing Company
califamedia.com
All Rights, Remedies & Liberties Reserved

Cover Photo:
Queen Califia and Her Amazons by Maynard Dixon
Located in the Room of the Dons, Mark Hopkins Hotel
San Francisco, California

"*A Nation can rise no higher than its woman*"
Hon. Elijah Muhammad f.k.a. Elijah Poole Bey

Table of Contents

PREFACE	I
I. INTRO	1
II. WHO ARE THE MOORS?	4
III. 77 AMAZING FACTS	8
PART 1 – AMAZING PEOPLE	8
PART 2 – AMAZING PLACES	39
PART 3 - AMAZING EVENTS & INFLUENCES	64
IV. NEED PROOF?	96
V. OUTRO	99
POST SCRIPT	103
WORKS CITED	104
TABLE OF FIGURES	106
OTHER TITLES FROM CALIFA MEDIA®	110

Preface

"Ethiopian and Moor were popularly used to describe so called blacks until 1500" (Rogers 1980).

Figure 1: J.A. Rogers
Source:
glogster.com/theshinyampharos/
joel-augustus-rogers

Peace and much respect to J.A. Roger for the information put forth in his book, *100 Amazing Facts about the Negro with Complete Proof*, originally published in 1934. This text, *77 Amazing Facts about Moors*, was patterned after Rogers' work. While we appreciate the works that he and other elders have put forth, it is time for the truth to be known.

i

1. Intro

Noble Drew Ali in his 101 Koran Questions for Moorish Americans, stated that Moors were not Negroes, blacks, colored, or Ethiopian, that we are made in the image and after the likeness of God, Allah[1] (Noble Drew Ali 2014). In the same text he also states that "Black, according to science, means Death"[2]. These are spiritual and Lawful statements.

Nigga, black, people of color, etc. These terms were created by man with the intention and the actual legal effect of imposing slavery. We understand what is meant by *black* on a social and cultural level. We know what our people mean when they say "black power". However, what we think words mean and our intended use don't magically change the words to actually mean what we imply....just because WE WANT them to.

Words have meanings, and they have meanings added on to their original definitions. This is the difference between denotative and connotative. Denotatively, *kid* means baby goat. Connotatively, we take *kid* to mean child. Just because we say kid and mean child does not change the fact that kid means baby goat. Likewise, just as we say *black* to mean our family, our people, our nation, etc., it does not change the fact that *black* scientifically means death.

When we voluntarily identify ourselves as black and Negro, legally, we are subjecting ourselves to slavery. African-American is comparable to the movie character Joe Dirt when he tried to switch his name to Joe "Deer-Tey". People tried to "pretty up" their slave status, but African-American, legally, means black, which means Negro, which means slave. According to the Law,

---

[1] Keys 90 and 91
[2] Key 87

Negroes, slaves, blacks nor African-Americans (this includes Latinos, Hispanics and Chicano) have rights in the United States because they are not legal citizens. In fact, according to all true and divine records of the human race, there is no Negro, black, or colored race attached to the human family.

> ***Jurisprudence***, *in* **LAW**, *is defined as "<u>the Science which treats of the principles of positive law and legal relations.</u>"* [3] (Black 1957).
>
> ***Civiliter Mortuus*** *in* **LAW**, *is defined as "<u>civilly dead; dead in the view of the law. The condition of one who has lost his civil rights and capacities, and is accounted dead in law.</u>"*[4] (Black 1957). *One who loses his civil rights is considered dead.*
>
> ***Negro*** *in* **LAW**, *is defined as "<u>a black man, one descended from the African race. Negro means necessarily a person of color, but not every person of color is 'negro'.</u>"* [5] (Black 1957).
>
> ***Color*** *in* **LAW**, *is defined as "<u>appearance, semblance, or simulacrum, as distinguished from that which is real. A deceptive appearance; a plausible, assumed exterior, concealing a lack of reality</u>. it also means <u>the dark color of the skin showing the presence of negro blood; and hence it is equivalent to African descent or parentage</u>"* [6]. (Black 1957)

As stated by the Prophet Noble Drew Ali, black according to science means death. Jurisprudence, the Science of Law, prove Ali's statement as True. "Black" People are people that appear to be real, but are not. Sort of like ghosts? But seriously, let us go deeper with this topic of Science. "Black" people are those who present themselves as being of Negro blood or equally, African descent. Therefore,

Black people = people of African descent = descendants of Negroes

---

[3] page 992
[4] page 312
[5] page 1188
[6] page 331

The importance of this is that what we feel is right, what we think is right, what we want to be right—according to Law—is not right. Negroes aka Blacks aka people with African descent aka African-Americans do not have rights. If you require further proof, see the over-ruled but not over-turned **Dred Scott Decision** (Scott v. Sandford 1857). This case went before the u.s. Supreme Court; the highest court in the land where it was confirmed that "black" people aka Negroes have no rights in this "country." Therefore,

Black people = civilly <u>dead</u>

In the u.s., being civilly dead means you have no civil rights. Don't you find it odd that "black" people are the ones marching for "civil rights"? Or why is there is no list of the civil rights for which we have been marching?

The truth is as El Hajj Malik El Shabazz said: "Civil Rights come with Human Rights. If you do not have Human Rights, you cannot have Civil Rights". We don't have civil rights as blacks because blacks are legally seen and treated as chattel property and as not human beings. The solution—our Liberty—comes from knowing the Truth.

The so called blacks, African-Americans, people of color, etc. are Moors!

Say it Loud, I'm Moor and I'm Proud!

Say it Loud, I'm Moor and I'm Proud!!

Say it Loud, I'm Moor and I'm Proud!!!

11. Who are the Moors?

The short answer is that the so called black people, brown people, African-Americans, Hispanics, niggas, people of color—all of these people are Moors. Our true name as a people was stripped from us and these imposed brand names or enslavement labels forced upon us. Over time, Knowledge of Self was forgotten and we truly believed we were Negroes, and then Blacks, and now African-Americans.

The programming has worked so well that most sleepy-headed Moors (those who still believe they are Black) will reject being called Moor in favor of a slave label. Active Moors have time and again heard many say, "Moor is a name the 'White' man (European) gave us" or "Moor means black". This section is for those still clinging to the enslavement labels or using the excuses mentioned above to prevent themselves and others from embracing our true heritage.

Before providing the definition for Moor, let us first examine the definition of blackamoor. According to the New Oxford American Dictionary, *blackamoor* is defined as "a black African; a very dark-skinned person". (Jewell 1998). The etymology section highlights blackamoor as a compound word, composed of the word *black* (the adjective or describing word) and *Moor* (the noun). However, this dictionary was published in 1998. Let us go back in time and see what the definition for blackamoor used to be. The American Dictionary of the English language, compiled in 1828 by Noah Webster defines blackamoor as "A negro, a black man". (Webster 1828). This entry is also recorded as a compound word, combining the individual terms *black* and *Moor*.

Here is a question that must be asked: If black-a-Moor is a compound word (meaning two words put together to create a new word), then how could Moor mean black? Wouldn't that be likened to saying black-a-black? What

4

about Moor-a-Moor? Neither of these terms make sense, do they? Intelligent consideration will lead the rational student to this conclusion. So, we are clear on the fact that Moor does not and cannot "mean" black as these are two different words with two different meanings. Let us also be clear though, that black is a term that has been used to substitute our correct and proper designation; Moor. Those people who have been known as "blacks" or "negroes" were being misrepresented. Those people were and are in fact, Moors.

Now let us examine the definition of Moor.

> **Moor** (mūəɹ, mōʊɹ), *sb.*² Forms: 4 Maur, 4-7 More, 5 Moure, Mowre, 6, 8 Maure, 6-7 Moore, 7- Moor. (Now with initial capital.) [ME. *More*, a. F. *More* (13th c.), *Maure*, ad. L. *Maurus* (med. L. *Mōrus*), Gr. Μαῦρος. Cf. Sp., Pg., It. *Moro*; MDu. *Moor, Moer* (Du. *Moor*), OHG. *Môr*, pl. *Môri* (MHG. *Môr, Mœr*, mod.G. *Mohr*).
> The L. *Maurus*, Gr. Μαῦρος may possibly be from some ancient North African language. Some believe the word to be merely a use of Gr. μαῦρος black (which on this view is aphetic from ἀμαυρός blind); but this adj. (or at least this sense of it) is confined to late Gr., and may even be derived from the ethnic name.]
>
> **1.** In *Ancient History*, a native of *Mauretania*, a region of Northern Africa corresponding to parts of Morocco and Algeria. In later times, one belonging to the people of mixed Berber and Arab race, Mohammedan in religion, who constitute the bulk of the population of North-western Africa, and who in the 8th c. conquered Spain. In the Middle Ages, and as late as the 17th c., the Moors were commonly supposed to be mostly black or very swarthy (though the existence of 'white Moors' was recognized), and hence the word was often used for 'negro'; cf. BLACKAMOOR.

Figure 2: Legal definition of Moor
Source Black's Law Dictionary 4ᵗʰ Deluxe Edition, 1951
dralimelbey.com

According to The New Oxford American Dictionary, Moor is defined as "A member of a Northwestern African Muslim people of mixed Berber and Arab descent. (Jewell 1998). In the 8th Century these people conquered the Iberian Peninsula, but were finally driven out of their last stronghold in

5

Granada at the end of the 15th Century (1492). The etymology section for the entry *Moor* states that the origin is "from Old French More, via Latin from Greek Mauros 'inhabitant of Mauretania'.

Webster's 1828 American Dictionary of the English language defines Moor as "A native of the northern coast of Africa, called by the Romans from the color of the people, Mauritania, the country of dark complexioned people. The same country is now called Morocco, Tunis, Algiers, &c. The etymology section states "Dutch or Belgic *moor;* German *mohr;* French *maure;* Greek *mavro,* meaning dark, obscure". (Webster 1828).

Based on the above, specifically, the Webster's 1828 definition, we can clearly see that the Moors are **NATIVE INDIGENOUS** people of the Northern or Northwestern Coast of Africa. Furthermore, unlike the enslavement term 'black' which gives a generic and intentionally vague connection to the land we call Africa, Moor connects us back to our History and cultures of Nations from the past, Morocco and Mauretania being two such examples. Superficial research into the history of Mauretania will reveal this nation was established as a kingdom in the 3rd Century B.C. More extensive research will lead you to connect Moors with Carthaginians, Phoenicians, Atlanteans, Moabites, and Muurs, to name a few.

Admittedly, a few of our Sisters and Brothers are still holding on to the enslavement brand "black," not unlike the elder in the film *Coming to America* with regard to use of Muhammad Ali's enslavement name. It is understandable where that urge comes from. It is human nature to want to hold onto what little culture we have left...or what we *think* is our culture. The truth is, when we let go of "black" and reclaim our true Moorish identity, we will regain our lost culture, history and then some!

One example is our homeland. When we decide to be who we are, to be ourselves—Moors—and proclaim it to the world, we will reclaim control of our land. What land does this refer to? All of what is known as the Americas. This is not limited to the territory those who occupy our land have been

6

referring to as America, but the entire Continent: from the top of North America, past Calgary and Toronto, through the so-called United States, south past Mexico, all the way to the tip of Argentina. This includes all of the islands of the Caribbean. Yes, all of this is the homeland and birthright of the Moors.

We are Moorish Americans, descendants of Moroccans, and born in America.

Now, let us give Black, Negro, and Colored back to the colonists and slave holders and be Ourselves!

It is time to uplift fallen humanity!

III. 77 Amazing Facts

Part 1 – Amazing People

1
Noble Drew Ali

launched the Moorish Divine and National Movement and founded the Canaanite Temple in the New Jersey territory in the year 1913 A.D.

Figure 3: Prophet Noble Drew Ali, Founder of the Moorish Science Temple of America, 1925

In 1925, Drew Ali would relocate the Temple's headquarters to Mecca (Chicago), shortly afterward adopting a new name-The Moorish Holy Temple of Science. The Temple's official name would be changed once more in 1926 to The Moorish Science Temple of America.

Prophet Noble Drew Ali prepared for the Moorish Americans the Holy Koran of the Moorish Science Temple of America (sometimes referred to the Circle 7 Koran) for their earthly salvation and to assist in the return to the ways of their ancient foremothers and forefathers.

Figure 5: Photo from first National Convention of the Moorish Science Temple of America. 1928

Figure 4: Prophet Noble Drew Ali surrounded by various dignitaries. 1928

Figure 6: Prophet Noble Drew Ali, 1925

Figure 7: Prophet Noble Drew Ali, Founder of Modern Islam in America

Figure 8: Noble Drew Ali sending the universal sign of distress on behalf of the Moorish Nation in America

2
Pearl Drew Ali

Sister Pearl Drews Ali was the wife of Prophet Noble Drew Ali. She was also instrumental in the founding the Young Peoples Moorish League, and worked as the National Secretary and Treasurer of the Moorish Science Temple of America and the Moorish Guide Newspaper.

Figure 9: Sis. Pearl Drew Ali.
Source: Sisters' Auxiliary Handbook, Califa Media 2014

3

Ruth

from the *biblios heliotech* (Bible) was a Moor. Our Ancient foremothers and forefathers were known as Moabites (as well as Canaanites, Hittites, and Amorites). There is an entire book dedicated to this Moorish woman that, among other things, documents her as the great-grandmother of King David, and an Ancestor of Jesus/Isa/ Yeshua. See Ruth 4:16. (The Holy Bible n.d.). Ruth is one of only two women in the entire Bible that has a book dedicated to her.

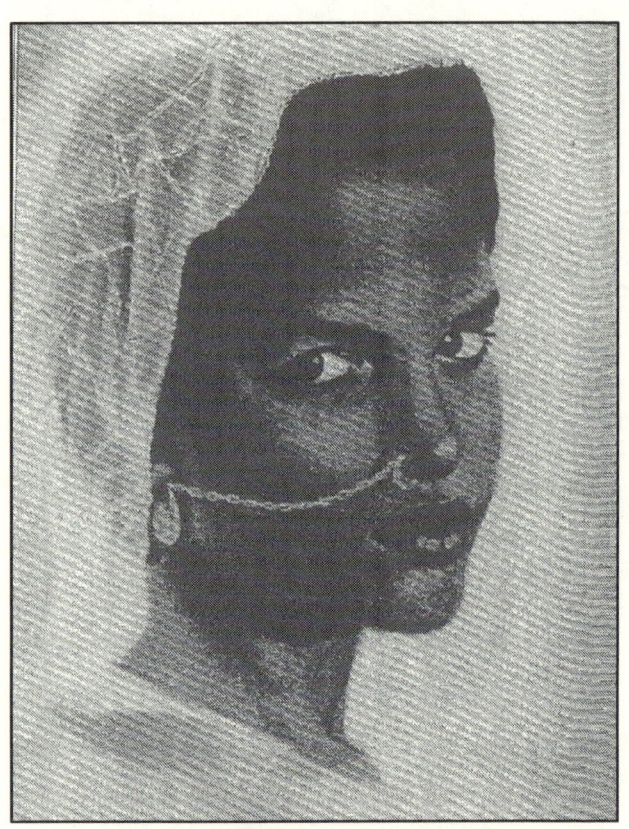

Figure 10: Depiction of Ruth the Moabitess.
Source: *aboriginalmoabitenation.co*

~ 4 ~
Isa Ibn Maryam [Jesus]

Jesus aka Yeshua ben Yosef aka Isa Ibn Maryam is a Moor was a direct descendant of the Canaanites and Moabites. The Moabite are the ancient ancestors of the Asiatics today known as Moors. All so-called black people are truly descendants of the same family line as the one known as Jesus. The image below (Fig. 11) is a piece done for the Legendary Hip Hop artist Cormega. It is a recreation of the biblical Last Supper, using Emcees in place of the traditionally know disciples. Tupac is the one who is representing Jesus.

Figure 11: Cover for Cormega's Album "Industry."
Source allhiphop.com

14

5
Saint Victor the Moor

A well-known Catholic saint from Africa, Victor Maurus or Saint Victor the Moor was born a Christian and served for a time in the Roman Praetorian Guard. Around 300 A.D., he was arrested, tortured and executed for his destruction of pagan shrines.

Figure 12: St. Victor the Moor.
Source: info.catholic.or.kr/saint/

◈ 6 ◈
Saint Benedict

is not only revered in Europe, but he is one of the most honored saints in all of South America. Known as Saint Benedict the Moor (hence the color of the statue pictured below), he remains highly respected throughout Europe.

Figure 14: St. Benedict the Moor.
Source: egyptsearch.com/

Figure 13: Marker for St. Benedict the Moor Catholic Church – Mother Church of Black Catholics in Georgia, Savannah, Georgia.
Source: lat34north.com/

** For all of our Sisters and Brothers who think being a Moor is about converting to Islam and becoming a Muslim or Moslem religiously, please know that there were many Moors who practiced what is known as "Christianity". Being a Moor is who we are by birth. It has little to do with what spiritual path or sacred texts you use as a guide in this journey called Life **

16

7
Marcus Opellius Macrinus

was a Roman Emperor. His origin was Mauretanian and he was known to be a Moor. It is said he descendent from an equestrian family and was versed in law, serving as legal advisor for the Praetorian Guard, director of traffic, financial advisor to a private estate and a Praetorian prefect. Through a series of serendipitous events, he was appointed emperor –and the first to not have served as a senator before assuming the position. He was overthrown and executed one year after becoming the Emperor in 217 A.D. (Roman Empire.Net n.d.).

Figure 15: Marcus Opellius Macrinus
(AD 164 - AD 218)
Source: thelifelonglearningacademy.com

8
Abu ʿAbdallah Muhammad XII

also known as King Boabdil, was the Sultan of Granada who surrendered to Fernidad and Isabella. This represented the defeat of the Moors and the end of our governing Europe. *End of Moorish rule in Europe.*

Figure 16: "Sigh of the Moor" by Marcelino de Unceta. Portrait of Moors exiting Al Andalus after the Fall of Granada. Source: egyptsearch.com.

18

9

Queen Califia

Legendary warrior-queen for whom the state of California is named, said to have led an army of women long ago when California was still a Pacific island.

"The name of Calafia was likely formed from the Arabic word khalifa (religious state leader) which is known as caliph in English and califain in Spanish." Source: Wikipedia.org "Calafia."

Figure 17: Califia, Queen of California
Source: TheAuthur Wright Portofolio
thearthurwright.net

~~10~~
Queen Sophia Charlotte

Research Queen Charlotte of Mecklenburg-Strelitz and you will quickly come across a historian called Mario de Valdes y Cocom. He argues that her features, as seen in royal portraits, were conspicuously Moorish, and contends that this fact was noted by numerous contemporaries. Valdes y Cocom claims that the queen, though German, was directly descended from a Moorish branch of the Portuguese royal family, related to Margarita de Castro e Souza, a 15th-century Portuguese noblewoman nine generations removed, whose ancestry traced from the 13th-century ruler Alfonso III and his lover Madragana. Valdes y Cocom contends Margarita was of Moorish descent and thus a black African. "If she, Queen Charlotte, was African," says the historian Kate Williams, "this raises a lot of important suggestions about not only our royal family but those of most of Europe, considering that Queen Victoria's descendants are spread across most of the royal families of Europe and beyond."

Figure 18: Duchess Sophia Charlotte of Mecklenburg-Strelitz.
Source: laura-cenicola.de

11

King Kalukaua

David La'amea Kamanakapu'u Mahinulani Nalaiaehuokalani Lumialani Kalākaua is also known as King Kalukaua. He was the last reigning King of the Kingdom of Hawaii prior to its forced annexation by the United States. Figure 19 shows His Majesty donning a Fez marked with the word Islam and a Shriner emblem.

Figure 19: His Majesty King Kalukaua
Source: sweetwatershrineclub.org

12

Estebanico

aka Estevanic, aka Esteban de Dorantes, aka Stephen the Moor, aka Mustafa Zemmouri, aka Esteban the Moor, a Moroccan. He is reported by some to be the first known person from Alkebulan (Africa) brought over to the Americas as an enslaved person. It is more likely he was one of those included when Isabella instructed Columbus to recruit his crew from the Spanish dungeons. Estabanico navigated the Americas as a guide for the European colonists for about 8 years (1500-1539).

Figure 20: Estavanico ("Esteban the Moor").
Source: tripdownmemorylane.blogspot.com

22

13

Sir Morien

was a knight thoroughly described in the romance novel, *The Hague Lancelot Compilation*. Morien is the son of Sir Agloval and a Moorish princess whom Agloval met in Africa during his quest to find the Holy Grail. Sir Morien is also described as a "bold knight" who experiences racism while seeking transportation overseas to reunite with his father, saying "None will take me over the water since I am a Moor."

Figure 21 Page from Moriaen
Source: images.frompo.com/i/morien-black-knight

23

14

The Waregem Moor

as depicted on the Waregem, Belgium coat of arms, is clearly an African king or someone of high nobility based on his clothing and golden crown atop his head. According to town history the present coat of arms was adopted in the 1970's after the merger of several smaller municipalities. This followed one adopted in the 1890s that featured what appears to be a "black faced," crowned Moor.

Figure 22: Coat of Arms for Waregem, West Flanders, Belgium.
Source: taneter.org/moorsheads.html

24

15
Beautiful Black

In the Estoria de Espanna (History of Spain), the first vernacular chronicle composed in Spain, we find a characteristic portrayal: "All the Moorish soldiers were dressed with silk and black wool that had been forcibly acquired ... their black faces were like pitch and the most handsome of them was as black as a cooking pan."

Figure 23: Depiction of the Battle of Badr.
Source: drrichswier.com

~~16~~

Berbers — *Inhabited the "Maghrib"*   *8,000,00 yrs. ago*

Those Berbers located in or near Tunisia were known as Numidians; farther to the west, the Berbers were called the Mauri or Maurisi (later the Moors). Moors together, with their relations and descendants, have been the major population group to inhabit the Maghrib (North African apart from the Nile) since about eight thousand years ago. This region includes terrain from the Nile to the Atlantic, encompassing the vast Sahara at whose center rise the mountain heights of Ahaggar and Tibesti. In the west the Mediterranean coastlands are suitable for agriculture, having for hinterland the Atlas Mountains.

Figure 24: Zenata Berebers of North Africa
Source: city-data.com

17
Barbary Moors

Europeans tell their own story in their own words about how they were shanghaied and taken back to North Africa as slaves. Over 2 million Europeans are reported to have been taken as slaves after being captured by Moors variously called Barbary Coast Pirates, Riff Pirates or Barbary Corsairs.

Figure 25: Cover of Charles Sumner's "White Slavery in the Barbary States." Source: Ostara Publications

Figure 26: Charles Sumner 1811-1874

18
Islamic Moros

(Figure 27: Photo of Moro Sultan of Talick and Datus (chieftain) circa 1904. Source: AfricareSource.com

Mutual revulsion between the Islamic Moros of the southern Philippines and the Western world has a long history. For more than two centuries before their defeat by U.S. forces at the end of the 1800s, Spain unsuccessfully attempted to subjugate the diminutive but fanatical Muslim Moros, who average slightly over 5 feet in height. Called Moros by the Spanish because they resembled Moroccan Moors who ruled Europeans for more than 700 years, the Moro tribes occupied—and still occupy—Mindanao; the second largest Philippine island, which is nearly the same size as Indiana.

Figure 28: Photo of Moro youth. circa 1904. Source: AfricareSource.com

The Island of Mindanao, Philippines

Figure 29: Mindanao, second largest and southernmost island of the Philippines.

19

The Sri Lankan Moors

possess a unique culture that differentiates them from the dominant Sinhalese and Tamil ethnic groups on the island. The Sri Lankan Moors have been strongly shaped by Islamic culture, with many customs and practices according to Islamic law. While preserving many of their ancestral customs, the Moors have also adopted several South Asian practices.

Figure 30: Ceylon Moors on Steps of Grand Mosque, New Moor Street, Colombo, Sri Lanka. 1901
Source: Puttalam Online

Abram Gannibal

the Moor of St. Petersburg, was perhaps the most famous African in Russian history. Brought to St. Petersburg from Istanbul by an agent of Russian tzar Peter the Great, he created for himself a brilliant military and civil career in the Russian Empire. He was educated in Europe where some say he befriended several famous French thinkers including Francois Diderot. Scientifically gifted and particularly talented in mathematics, he is perhaps best known today as the great-grandfather of Alexander Pushkin. (G.S. Salaam El 2014)

Figure 31: Portait of Gannibal by Eugene Delacroix
Source: Frontarad Digital Magazine
frontarad.com

Figure 32: Memorial of Gannibal.
Source: stephenhicks.org

31

𝒟use 𝔐ohamed 𝒜li

Figure 33: Duse Mohammed Ali. Source: "Nationality, the Order of the Day" by G.S. Kudjo Adwo El

was invited to attend the Universal Races Congress in 1911, at the University of London. Although a thousand people attended, only a small portion were from the African Diaspora. Ali did, however, meet with W.E.B. Du Bois at this conference. (GS. Adwo El 2014)

** The Honorable Marcus Mosiah Garvey (Fig. 34) is acknowledged and respected as the forerunner to Prophet Noble Drew Ali. He was mentored by and worked with Duse Mohamed Ali in the early 1900s**

Figure 34: Hon. Marcus Garvey. Source: "Nationality, the Order of the Day" by G.S. Kudjo Adwo El

22

Charles Mosley Bey

a Moorish Master Astrologer, founder of the Clock of Destiny Moorish National order in 1947. He authored *Clock of Destiny I* and *II*, and the *Circle of Life*. Mosely Bey went on to register his works, most notably the *Zodiac Constitution*, with the Library of Congress for the United States of America in 1947, coded at U.S. Code Title 22 Chapter 2 Sec. 141 under judicial protection.

Figure 35: "About C.M. Bey."
Source rvbeypublications.com

El Hajj Malik El Shabazz

"Malcolm X" is known in North America as one of the greatest "black" Revolutionaries of the 20th Century. A rarely acknowledged fact by many is that his true name was El Hajj Malik El Shabazz. El, the shortened singular of *Eloah* and the plural *Elohim*, is one of our Moorish Titles.

*Figure 36: El Hajj Malik El Shabazz at the Great Pyramids.
Source: problackempowerment.com*

24

Afrika Bambaataa Bey

is one of the founders of our Indigenous Moorish culture known as Hip Hop and the Universal Zulu Nation. Bambaataa Bey made a Moorish Hip Hop Proclamation in New York in March of 2014. He stated that the so called black and brown people are Indigenous Moors, who spread our art all over the mighty Earth. Peace to DJ Kool Herc and all of the Elders, Legends, and Founders of Hip Hop. And a special shout out to KRS-One for the Gospel of Hip Hop.

Figure 37: Founders of HipHop being honored in front of New York City Hall. Afrika Bambaataa Bey center, in beads. Source: nydailynews.com

25

Stevie Wonder

is an amazing artist. In his song *Misrepresented People* from the soundtrack for the film Bamboozled, he sang this amazing lyric: "In 1492 you came upon these shores. / Seven hundred years, educated by the Moors." Even more amazing is that his legal name is Stevie Morris, Morris being a name that connects him directly back to our Moorish Heritage.

Figure 38: Image of Stevie Wonder from the early 1970s wearing shirt with Zodiac glyphs. Source: discogs.com

Figure 39: Album cover for the soundtrack to the film Bamboozled. Source: discogs.com.

26

Yasiin Bey

formely known as Mos Def, is from the Brooklyn territory of North Amexem. He is a world renowned Artist, musically as well as in acting. On the album artwork of the back cover of Yasiin Bey's album "The Ecstatic" is an image of Noble Drew Ali and other Moorish Americans in front of a home in the late 1920s. (G.S. Salaam El 2014)

*Figure 40: Back panel of Yasiin Bey's "The Ecstatic" album.
Source: "Moorish Jewels-Emerald Edition" by Rami Salaam El*

27
Nas aka Nastradamus

is from the Queensbridge territory of North Amexem. In his song, "Y'all my Niggas", he said, "...The problem is we started thinking like the colonists, 'Til Noble Drew Ali started droppin' that consciousness..."

Figure 41: Musical legends Damian Marley, and Nas performing their amazing collaborative album, Distant Relatives.
Source: pastemagazine.com

Part 2 – Amazing Places

Mu

In ancient times, Moors were known as Muurs. About 50,000 years ago, we inhabited a country called Mu. It was located to the West of the North America continent, but is now rumored to be at the bottom of the ocean. Mu is called the "original Garden of Eden" by James Churchward in his book, "The Lost Continent of Mu" and an ancient map of Mu from his book is provided (Fig. 42). The selection to follow provides a current map of Rapa Nui or Easter Island so the reader can compare where it is in relation to the Map of Mu.

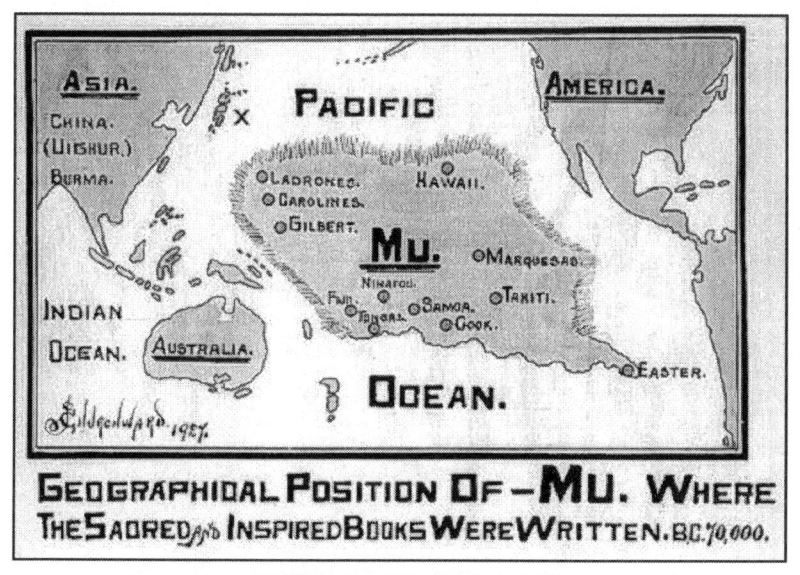

Figure 42: 1927 sketch of Mu by Col. J. Churchward.
Source: atlantisforschung.de

ꙮ 29 ꙮ
𝓡apa 𝓝ui [𝓔aster 𝓘sland]

Remnants of ancient stone statues arrayed in fezzes are located on the island named Rapa Nui. The statues themselves have been named "Moai" and there are an estimated 900 of them on the island, the largest being 71 feet high and weighing approximately 170 tons. Most mainstream "scientists" and "researchers" claim they have no idea how the statues got here, and who could have created them.

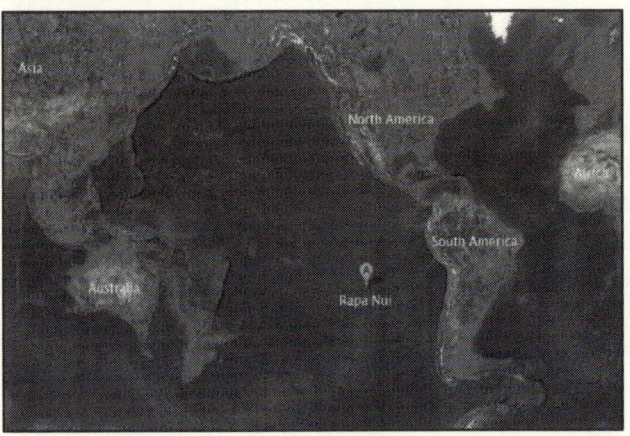

Figure 43: Satellite image of Rapa Nui.
Source: Google Earth

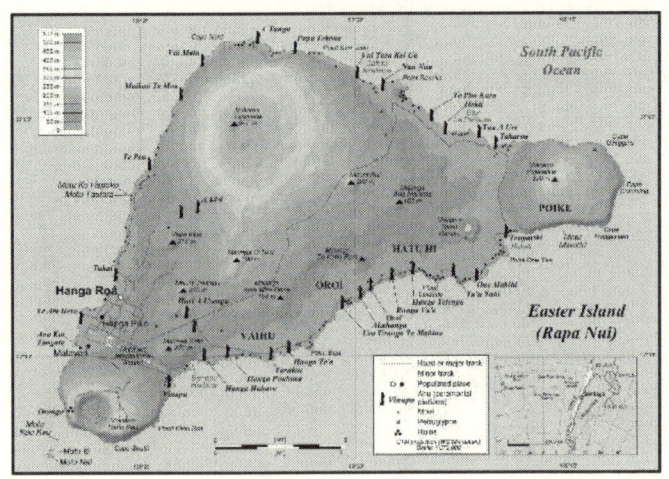

Figure 44: Map of Rapa Nui showing statue sites.
Source: memographer.com

** The following images are provided as a reference to show the reality of how massive these statutes truly are. Interestingly, in the film *Atlantis: The Lost Empire*, there are gigantic stone statutes that are Guardians of the land and people**

Figure 46: Stand of "Moai".
Source: historyworlds.ru

Figure 45: Perspective rendering for Moai Tuturi (l) and Moai Ahu Tongariki (r).
Source: allmysteryworld.blogspot.com

Figure 47: Body of Moai statue.
Source: taringa.net

30

The Mauryan Empire

was the first great empire of the Indian sub-continent, and that in itself gives it major importance in world history. It was one of the great empires of the ancient world; in size at least it was on a par with the Persian, Roman and Han empires.

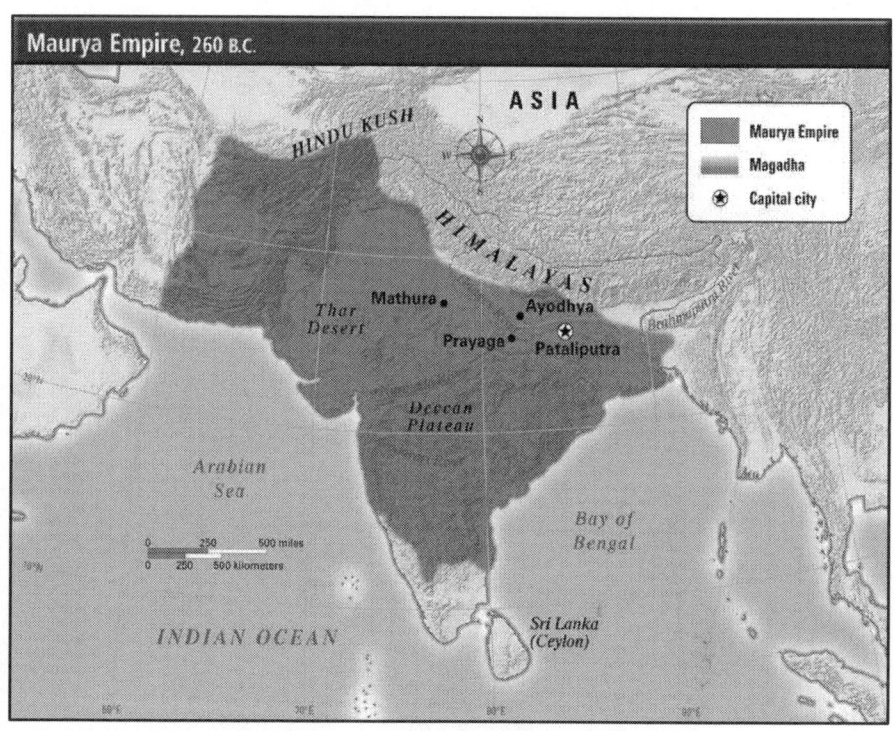

Figure 48: Mauryan Empire under Ashoka.
Source: indiandefence.com

31
The Temple Mount

is one said to be of the most important religious sites in Jerusalem (Of the East). Adherents to Islam, Christianity and Judaism have used this site for religious purposes over thousands of years. One of the Gates to the Temple is named The Moroccans Gate, Mughrabi Gate, or very plainly, the Gate of the Moors. This particular gate is the only entrance to the Temple for those who don't claim to be Muslims. (Jerusalem Virtual Tours 2009).

Figure 49: Temple Mount, Jerusalem
Source: Wikipedia.org, image by Andrew Shiva

Figure 50: Dome of the Rock, Temple Mount, Jerusalem
Source: Wikipedia.org, image by Chris Flook

45

32

Mauritania

is Latin for "land of the Moors", named after classical Mauretania in northern Morocco, itself named after the Berber Mauri or Moor tribe. The Senegalese "Moors," although of northern origin and calling themselves former vassals of the Emperor of Morocco, have nothing but their name, language and religion in common with the Mauritanian Moors.

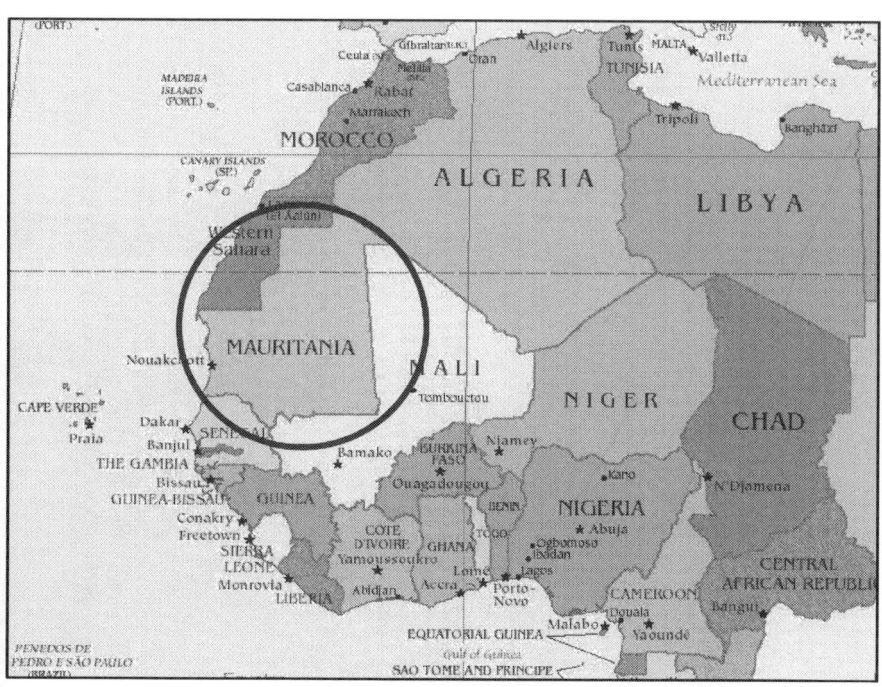

Figure 51: Political map of North Africa, Mauritania circled.
Source: projekt-benin.de

~~ 33 ~~
Mecca, the Kabba and the Seven

Our Moorish ancestors were the founders of the city of Mecca, or as it was known in ancient times, Bakkah. The black cube seen in the image below is called the Kaaba, and is the holiest site in Mecca and Islam. It is in the center of what is known as the most sacred Mosque, Al-Masjid Al-Haram. Tawaf is a custom practiced among Muslims in which they walk around the Kaaba Seven times, demonstrating the unity of believers in the worshipping of Allah.

Figure 53: Holy Kabbah (circled) in Mecca, Arabia. Source: google.com

Figure 52: The Logos 7/ Broken Seventh Seal

34

Al Andalus

Jews and Christians lived in peace under Moorish Moslem rule in Iberia—more-so than in any part of Europe at that time. This 700 year period marked a Golden Age in Europe; ending their Dark Age and preceding their Renaissance.

Figure 54: Al Andalus at its height of power on the Iberian Penninsula. Source: museumofthecity.org

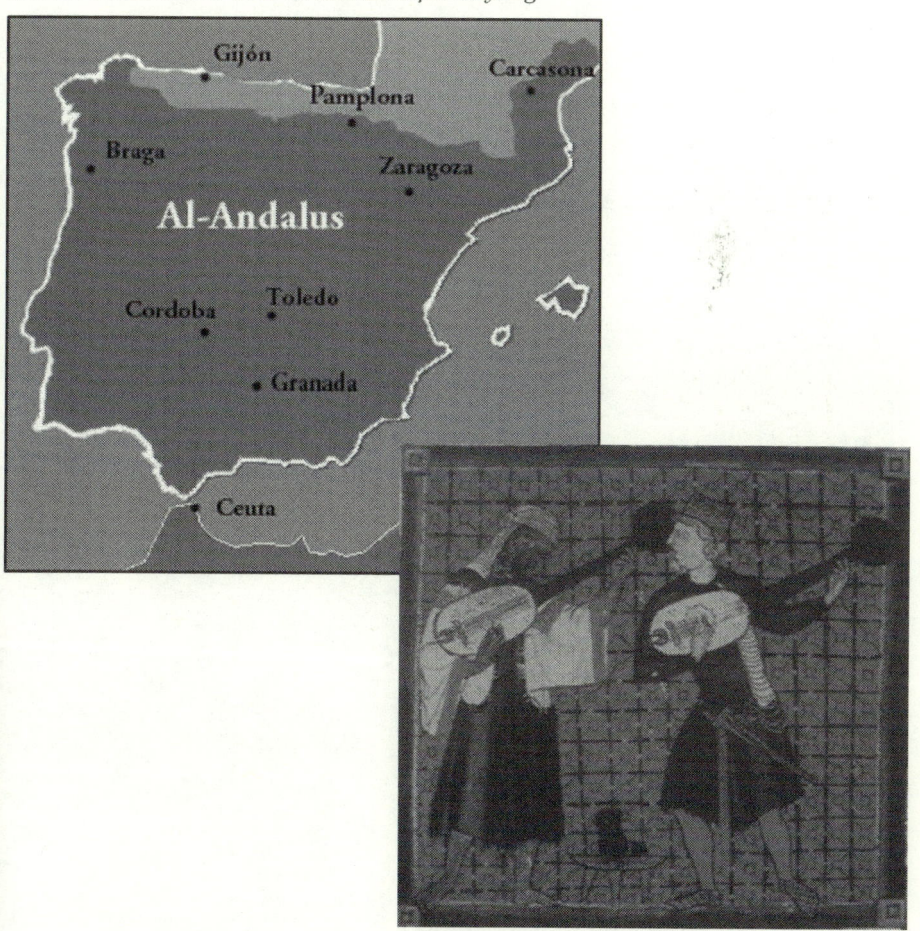

Figure 55: Moslem and Christian playing music. Source: museumofthecity.org

❦ 35 ❧
The Generalife Gardens

are probably the best known gardens in Spain. Located on the grounds of the Alhambra Palace, they are known for their vast size and the joy one experiences when walking through them. At the entrance, there is a large open air patio that slopes to a stage where concerts and other public performances are held. Everywhere there are little fountains that splash water. The sound of running water was very soothing to the Moors and they engineered a system to bring large amounts from the Darro River upstream from the city of Granada to the Alhambra fortress. This served the additional function of enabling them to withstand sieges when water may not have been accessible.

Figure 57: The Ladies Pond.
Source: imarabe.org

Figure 56: Patio del Canale
Source: zloris.blogspot.com

Fountain of the Lions

The Alhambra Palace has the Fountain of the Lions; an ancient symbol that arrived in Granada from pre-Christian civilizations in the East. The lion spewing water from its mouth is the sun, which gives life to everything. The 12 suns of the fountain represent the 12 stations of the zodiac, and the 12 months of the year.

Figure 59: Patio de los Leones, Nasrid Palace, Alhambra.
Source: zloris.blogspot.com

Figure 58: Close-up of the Fountain of Lions.
Source pixels.com

50

~~ 37 ~~
The Asiatic Nations of North, Central, and South America

such as the Mexicans, Brazilians, Argentinians, Chilians, Columbians, Nicaraguans, the natives of San Salvador, the Moorish Americans, etc., all of these people are Moors. (Noble Drew Ali, The Holy Koran of the Moorish Science Temple of America Circle 7 1928) Yes, from the top of the map (Fig. 21), all the way to the bottom, and all the surrounding islands. All of the indigenous peoples of this land are Moors. We are all family!

Figure 60: Moorish Empire in the West

38

Tlachihualtepetl

or Great Pryamid of Cholula, is the Largest Pyramid in the world known to the masses today. The Third Largest Pyramid of the Sun is 90 meters away. A few miles from that is the Pyramid of the Moon. All three of these Pyramids are in Central America. (Skhs. Najee-Ullah El 2014).

Figure 61: Photo of the Pyramid of the Moon taken from the Pyramid of the Sun.

39

The New York City Center

a performance house for major dance companies including the Fall for Dance Festival, features a distinct Moorish Revival style.

The Center was originally built in 1923 as the Mecca Temple; a meeting place for members of a specific Masonic order.

Figure 62: Facade of New York City Center, Manhattan, NY. Source: love4musicals.com.

40

The Central Synagogue

remains the crown jewel of the Manhattan Moorish Revival. Dating from 1872 (making it the oldest synagogue in continuous use), its beauty actually came under criticism in earlier days by those who felt its excess would inspire envy.

Figure 63: Central Synagogue, Manhattan, NY.
Source: snipview.com

41
Noble Drew Ali Plaza

In the Brownsville area of New York Territory, there was a housing complex named after Prophet Noble Drew Ali. It was purchased by Omni New York and, according to an interview with the Russian co-founder of Omni, Eugene Schneur, champion boxer Mike Tyson knew about the complex and lived a few blocks away. Unfortunately, the current "owners" of the buildings are not dealing with the community honorably.

*Figure 64: Image of Noble Drew Ali Plaza.
Source: nydailynews.com*

42

The Moor's Indian Charity School

was founded in Lebanon, Connecticut, in 1754 by Eleazar Wheelock. His plan was to remove Indian children from their homelands in order to educate and convert them so that they could return to their societal groups and teach their own people. He believed his plan was divinely sanctioned as the best defense against hostilities between the Indians and colonists.

Figure 65: Placard for Moor's Charity School, Columbia, CT. Source: historicbuildingsct.com.

43

Palestine, Illinois

There are two towns in North America named Palestine: one in Texas established in 1846, the other in Illinois founded in 1678. According to the city history website page, this oldest town in Illinois was named Palestine when the French explorer Jean Lamotte saw the land, saying it reminded him of the promised land of "milk and honey." (City of Palestine 2010).

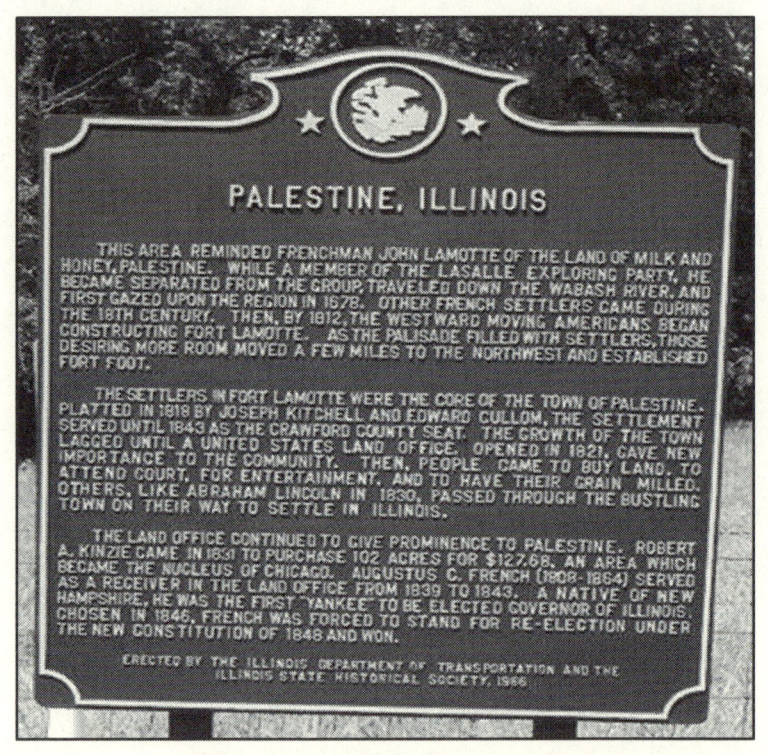

Figure 66: Marker for City of Palestine, Illinois.
Source: pioneercity.com

In ancient times their land too was referred to as Canaan. This connects us back to our brothers and sisters in the Palestine of the East. Their nation too is currently occupied by a foreign government.

Moab, Utah

a town in North America, was established in 1878. This Western location connects us with our ancient ancestors, the Moabites, who inhabited the area of land near the Jordan River in the East, which they named Moab. (Jackson El 2015).

*Figure 67: Moab, Utah city marker.
Source: moab.utahsbusinessdirectory.com.*

Fox Oakland Theatre

is known for the Moorish influence in it's design and structure. Its style is likened that of a medieval Castle. Some have quoted it as being reminiscent of a Brahmin Temple and initially, developers considered naming it just that. In the 1920s, the Fox Theatre was one of **the** theaters to visit on the West Coast. (Oaktown Art 2010).

Figure 68: Fox Oakland Theater. Telegraph Avenue facade with marquee

*Figure 69: Pylons of Fox Oakland Theater
Source: oaktownart.com.*

*Figure 71: Front view of Fox Oakland Theater
Source: oaktownart.com.*

*Figure 70: Windows of Fox Oakland Theater
Source: oaktownart.com.*

~~ 46 ~~

Mauritania Avenue

is a street in Bey Area territory of Califia, Amexem (commonly known as Oakland, California, North America). This connects the NorthWest coast of Amexem with the nation of Mauritania on the Northwest coast Alkebulan (Africa). The history of Moors inhabiting that nation and area date back over a thousand years to the 3rd century.

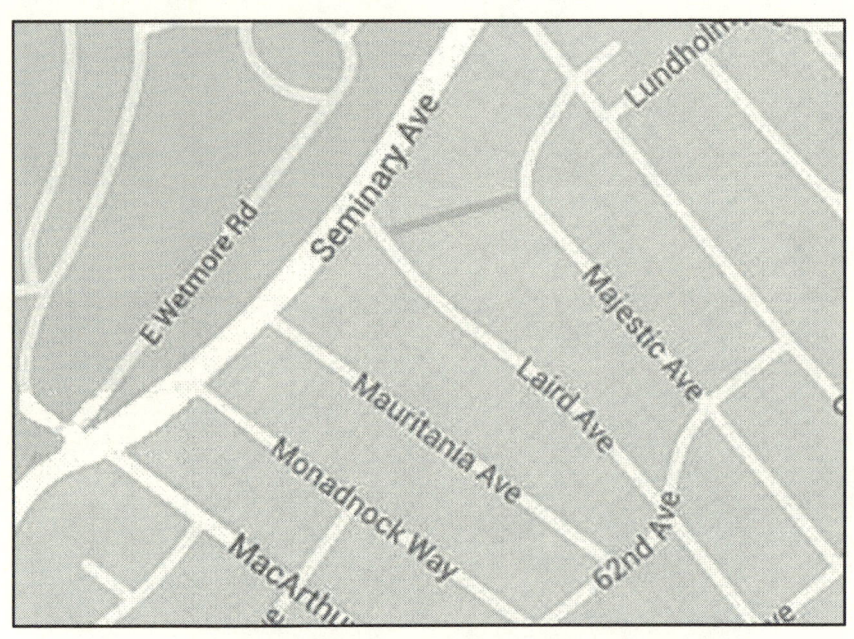

Figure 72: Map of Mauritania Avenue, Oakland California. Image sourced from Google Maps

Morro Bay

is a town in in Southern California established in 1870. At this location, there is a formation called Morro Rock which is referenced as the Gibraltar of the Pacific. (Morro Bay.com 1995). Our Moro (Filipino) brothers and sisters were documented as living here as far back as the late 1500s.

Morro Rock is a geologic formation said to be the plug of a volcano. It is still considered a sacred space to local indigenous and used in annual solstice rituals.

Figure 73: Morro Rock.
Image by Kjkolb, 2006.
Sourced from Wikipedia Creative Commons

48
The Canaanite Temple

set aside by Noble Drew Ali in 1913. This was the first Temple on record that Noble Drew Ali established for the Moors of North Amexem. It was founded in 1913, in the Newark, New Jersey territory.

Figure 74: The Canaanite Temple.
Source: "Moorish Jewels Emerald Edition"

Part 3 - Amazing Events & Influences

49
Custodians of Egyptian Culture

Moors were the people who preserved the ancient knowledge of Egypt during the Persian, Greek, and Roman invasions of Alkebulan (Africa). Egyptians were family, so it only made sense to prevent the destruction of our Brothers and Sisters culture by invading foreigners. Metaphysics, natural sciences (such as astronomy, astrology, alchemy), writing, mathematics, philosophy, were among the teachings protected by the Moors.

According to *Stolen Legacy* by George G.M. James, Moors were the ones who took the wisdom teachings (also known as *sophia*) and spread this knowledge into large parts of Africa, Asia Minor, and Europe. James goes on to say that the Moors were the people that the world looked to for enlightenment and points out that prophets from Moses to Christ (Jesus aka Isa)—and we may now include Noble Drew Ali—were ALL Initiates in the Egyptian Mystery System.

Obviously there is a contradiction by using African-American and Black when the true name Moor is in plain sight, but this just goes to show how the blatant de-nationalization and enslavement programming is in the u.s.

Figure 75: Cover of "Stolen Legacy" originally published 1954.
Source atlantablackstar.com

50

The Other Red, Black, and Green

Our Moorish Flag, all red with a five pointed green star representing Love, Truth, Peace, Freedom, and Justice (and outlined in black), is over 10,000 years old! This, by association, means that the Nation and the people have been here in Amexem for over 10,000 years as well.

"Moros"

The term Moro was not derogatory or pejorative when first used by the Spaniards. It was derived from the first four letters of country of origin of the conquerors of Spain – Morocco –"Moro" (singular or Moros - plural form), or "Moor" (singular and Moors – plural) in English. The first mention of the term Moro in Spanish records refers to a trader who became the interpreter of Ferdinand Magellan to Rajah Humabon of what is today known as the Philippines. This Moro must have traveled extensively for he even warned the Cebuanos (also of the Philippines) that the Spaniards are mighty warriors. He may have been an Arab trader for never was he mentioned as a native practicing Islam, and the Philippines was then a transit point for Arab merchants on their way to China.

*Figure 76: Los Moros.
Source friki.net*

52

Moors Introduced Chess

to Europeans in the 800s. History reveals that Moorish Caliph Harun Al Rashid gave Charlemagne, who was the first emperor of the Roman Empire, a chess set. By the year 1000, the game spread through all of Europe. Do some research into the ancient game Chess evolved from, Chaturanga. By the year 1000, the game of Chess spread through all of Europe.

Figure 77: Earliest known depiction of a game of chess. Source: chess.com

53

Advancements in Agriculture

Under the Moors, Spain was introduced to new food crops such as rice, hard wheat, oranges, lemons, sugar and cotton. More importantly, along with these foodstuffs came an intimate knowledge of irrigation and cultivation of crops. The Moors also taught the Europeans how to store grain for up to 100 years and built underground grain silos.

IBN-AL-AWAM*
A SOIL SCIENTIST OF MOORISH SPAIN

LOIS OLSON AND HELEN L. EDDY

TWO hundred years ago the "Kitab al-Felahah" or "Book of Agriculture,"[1] of Ibn-al-Awam was rediscovered in the Royal Spanish Library of San Lorenzo del Escorial and hailed as the greatest of all medieval treatises on agriculture. For hundreds of years this work had been completely lost to the Spanish farmers for whom it had been written in the latter half of the twelfth century of our era. Other European countries had never heard of Ibn-al-Awam. The earlier Roman agricultural writings, including those of Spanish-born Columella, had been preserved in monastery libraries, but Ibn-al-Awam was a Moor. As long as the conflict between the Moors and the Christians remained fresh in their memories, church and state alike condemned everything Moorish, even their agricultural achievements. It must be remembered that the first Moorish invaders had found little remaining of the highly developed agriculture of Roman Spain; for the Goths had been in possession of the country for three hundred years when, in A.D. 711 the Moorish invasion swept over the peninsula.

While the rest of Europe was passing through the darkest period of the Middle Ages, Moorish cities were growing in wealth and power. Córdoba became a center of learning that attracted scholars from all parts of the world. The library there is said to have contained 600,000 volumes, including Arabic translations of the classics of Rome and Greece. By the eleventh century Spain was producing its own scientific literature, in caliber rivaling, and in some ways surpassing, that of Rome. Among the Moorish writers agriculture was a favorite subject because of its religious implications. According to tradition, Mohammed himself said: "Whosoever plants

---

* This paper is one of a series on pioneer soil conservationists of the western Mediterranean region. Others included in the series are Cato, Vergil, Columella, Pietro de Crescenzi, Leonardo da Vinci, and the Paulini brothers of Venice.

Figure 78: Except from journal paper on Ibn Al-Awam, Geographical Review Jan. 1943.

Source: jstor.org

54

Moorish Logic

At a time when Europe had only two universities, the Moors had seventeen, located in Almeria, Cordova, Granada, Juen, Malaga, Seville, and Toledo. Under Moorish rule, education was universal and available to all. In the 10th and 11th centuries, public libraries in Europe were non-existent, while Moorish Spain could boast of more than 70, including one in Cordova that housed hundreds of thousands of manuscripts. Universities in Paris and Oxford were established after visits by scholars to Moorish Spain.

Figure 79: "The Connoisseurs."
Source: "Moorish Jewels-Emerald Edition" by Rami Salaam El

55

Moors in Literature

By 800 AD, the Franks began efforts to contain the spread of Moorish society to the south of the Pyrennees Mountains. Much of the literature, lore and art that followed centered on the Franks' efforts to defeat the Moors. The Song of Roland (French, La Chanson de Roland, 1140- 1170 AD), the oldest known French literary work, describes Frankish Charlemagne's (742-814 AD) long campaign in southern France against a Moorish leader named Marsile.

> In the 'Chanson of Roland' (Song of Roland) written after the Moors invaded France in 718 A.D., the invaders are described (verses 145 and 146) as "blacker than ink with large noses and ears" and with "nothing white except the teeth." (Moriaen. Arthurian Romance No. 4, PP. 29, 39, 41, 103. 1907. Trans. by J. L. Watson). The Chanson of Roland states that the Moorish army was 50,000 strong and led by Marganice, Emperor of Ethiopia and Carthage. Their most valiant figure is Abisme (that is, Abyssinian), who (verse 126) is described as "black as melted pitch." In this epic, the Moors are called Sarrazins, in English, Saracens. (Spider879 2013).

Figure 80: Depiction of scene from "The Song of Roland."
Source: abovetopsecret.com

Moorish Math

The Moors originated Algebra and developed Trigonometry into a science used all around the world. The word Algebra is derived from "Al-Jabr wa'l Muqabala," the title of the first textbook on the subject. We also get the word algorithm (a math procedure) from the Moors.

The Arabic numbers we use today come from the ancient Arab people who are known historically as Moors.

Figure 81: Sample of Moorish use of math in interior design. Source: alexeflier.com

Form, Function and Fractals

The use of geometry in decor was a nod to the Moors' talent in structural design and mathematics. The Koran forbids the copying of natural forms so instead craftsman used stars, crescents, crosses, hexagons and octagons. (Moslems/ Muslims were not allowed to depict human figures, animals and flowers in their designs.) These geometric shapes and patterns were created in wood, plaster, tile and textile designs and these colors used in their designs: red, blue, green, white, silver and gold. The Moorish influence on design is one that acutely reflects the religious and topographical influences of Islam and Spain. The interior elements of these buildings - horseshoe & scalloped arches, stalactites, simple columns and multi foils - are exquisite and unique.

Figure 82: Sample of the use of fractals in Moorish design. Source mattsko.worpress.com

58
"Arabesque" Architecture

Authorities believe that Arabian glass windows appeared in the second half of the thirteenth century. Lewis F. Day suggests that Byzantine, Moorish or Arabian glass could have appeared by the tenth century AD. Arabian filigree windows moved into Europe when the Moors entered Spain.

Figure 83: University of Tampa's Plant Hall. Source ut.edu.

~~ 59 ~~
Moors as Art

The contributions of the Moors will forever be remembered through Moor's heads which appear all over Europe--as paintings, statues, and on the official coats of arms (and flags) of municipalities, religious groups, and noble families. It's important to note the Europeans often portrayed Moors in a positive light -- often adorning them with crowns and jewelry.

Figure 86: Codognato broche of Moor- engraved gold, silver & gem stones.
Source alaintruong.com

Figure 85: Moorish broche by Cartier. Source es.paperblog.com

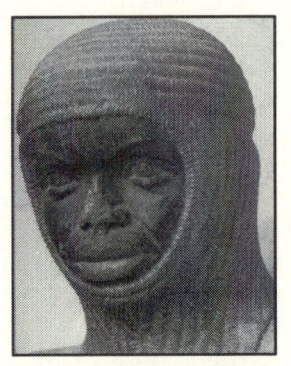

Figure 84: Statue of Moorish knight in chainmail armor.
Source: abovetopsecret.com

75

🙢 60 🙠
The Coat of Arms of Škofja Loka

is "Vert on a base sable a gate or in entrance a Moor's head sable crowned gules". The Moor's head is common element in the arms and seals of various towns that were under the rule of the diocese of Freising (Bavaria, Germany) throughout Central Europe. The use of the head within the gates in the seal of Škofja Loka is confirmed at least from 1471.

Figure 87: Coat of Arms from Loka Castle Škofja Loka Museum.
Source anjaperse.com

61

The Mauryan Period

of Indian history was really inaugurated by the conquest of northwest India by Alexander the Great, in 326 BC. This seems to have destabilized the political situation amongst the Aryan states in the region, and provided an opportunity for the first great conqueror in Indian history, Chandragupta Maurya (reigned 322-298 BC), to rise to power. Chandragupta seized control of the throne of Maghada from the last Nanda king, and then proceeded to conquer that part of northern India which still remained outside Magadha's borders. He drove out Alexander's successors from the Indian subcontinent, and went on to conquer the easternmost provinces of Alexander's former empire, reaching into Afghanistan and eastern Iran. Internally, building on foundations laid by the Nanda kings, his reign saw the establishment of a strong central government.

Figure 88: Chandragupta Maurya, founder of the Maurya Empire.
Source ancient.eu.

62

Perdida de España

The earliest European account of the Moorish invasion of Spain, the Chronicle of 754, refer to the Visigothic capitulation, the so-called "loss of Spain" (perdida de España) at the hands of the "Arabs and Moors sent by Musa," or Musa Ibn Nusayr, the Muslim governor of North Africa.

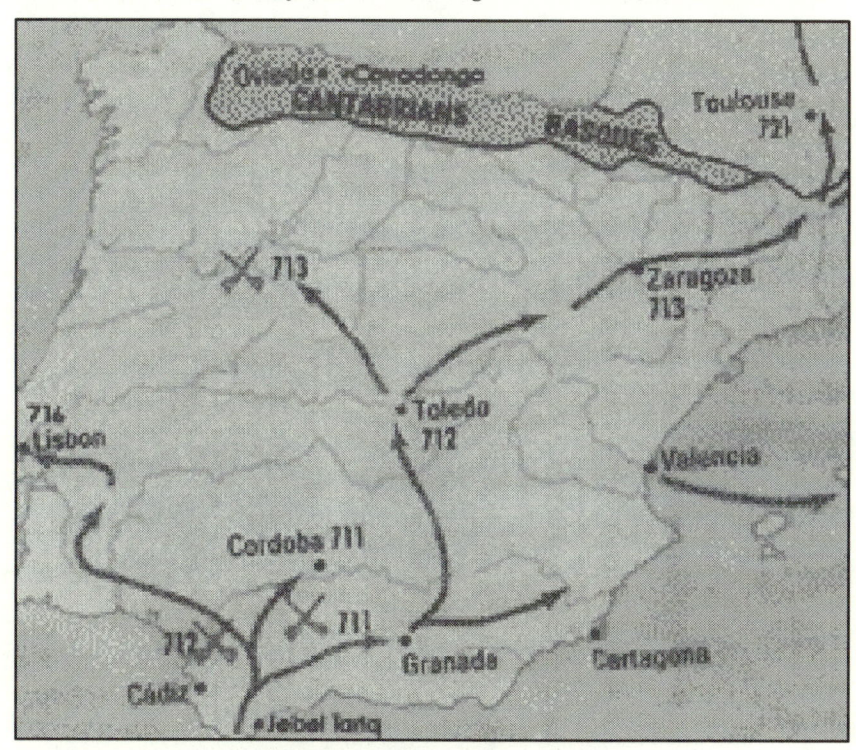

Figure 89: *Expansion of Moors into the Iberian Peninsula.*
Source: *northsouthguides.com*

April Fools' Day

The origin of April Fools' Day is nothing to laugh about. It is reported that on April 1st, 1492, deception on the part of Europeans (Christians) resulted in the slaughter of hundreds Moors. During the fall of their European empire, Moors being expelled from Spain were offered boats to take them back Morocco. When our ancestors headed for the boats, the Christians burned the homes they left behind and sunk the ships, leaving our people caught to be viciously murdered. (Moon 2004).

64

Operacion Colombo

Christopher Columbus records numerous examples of Moors already present in the Americas. He commented on the gold that the natives had, which was made the same way, in the same alloy, as the Muslims of West Africa.

Figure 90: Columbus on his arrival on Hispaniola.
Source: trans-caribbean.blogspot.com

~~ 65 ~~

England vs. Moors

In 1596, Queen Elizabeth issued an "open letter" to the Lord Mayor of London, announcing that "there are of late divers blackmoores brought into this realm, of which kind of people there are already here too many," and ordering that they be deported from the country. One week later, she reiterated her "good pleasure to have those kind of people sent out of the land" and commissioned the merchant Casper van Senden to "take up" certain "blackamoores here in this realm and to transport them into Spain and Portugal." Finally, in 1601, she complained again about the "great numbers of Negars and Blackamoors which (as she is informed) are crept into this realm," defamed them as "infidels, having no understanding of Christ or his Gospel," and again authorized their deportation.

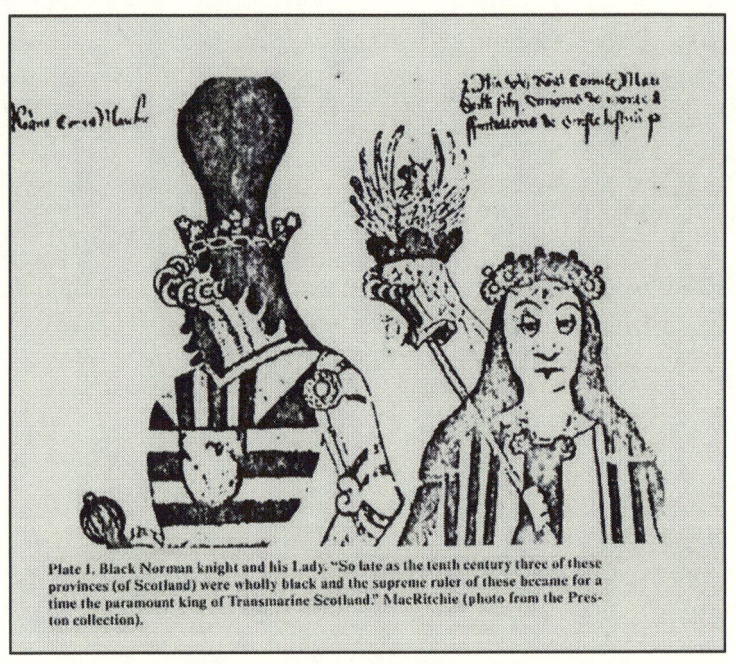

Plate 1. Black Norman knight and his Lady. "So late as the tenth century three of these provinces (of Scotland) were wholly black and the supreme ruler of these became for a time the paramount king of Transmarine Scotland." MacRitchie (photo from the Preston collection).

Figure 91: From the collection of Sir. Thomas Wriorthesley / cover of Ancient and Modern Broitons by D. Mac Ritchie.
Source: blackpresence.blogspot.com

66
Moros y Christianos

is a famous Cuban food dish. It means Moors and Christians, and it features black beans for the Moors, and white rice for the Christians.

*Figure 92: Serving of moros y christianos.
Source: customcatering.net*

67
U.S. vs. Moros

The Spanish colonisers never succeeded in subjugating the Moro sultanates. However, when Spain ceded the Philippines to the US in 1898, the Moro homeland, Bangsamoro, was included. Isolated fighting took place in 1901 and was renewed in the spring of 1903. US troops were attacked near Lake Lanao in the interior of Mindanao. The best known of the U.S corporation-Moro battles occurred in March 1906 at the top of Mount Dajo on the island of Jolo. Moro who had taken refuge inside a large volcanic crater were killed by troops under Gen. Leonard Wood. As usual a number of women and children were killed. Wood came under severe criticism in the U.S. Congress, but he was absolved of any wrongdoing by Pres. Theodore Roosevelt. In the ensuing war, which lasted until 1913, 20,000 Moros — fighters and civilians — were killed.

Figure 93: Image from Bud Dajo Massacre, 1906.
Source: xiaochua.net

68
The .45 Caliber Bullet

came into common use during the early 1900s. The u.s. Army was trying to conquer the Moros, but the .38 caliber bullet was not strong enough to kill them, so they upgraded their weaponry. They even went so far as to hang our Filipino brothers and sisters. Look into what is labeled as the Tagalog [Philippine] -American war".

Please note that the u.s. democracy does not, and never did represent the true Americans, but have been using our name to cause terror and chaos all over the world.

Figure 94: Moro warriors circa 1900.
Source: mrcheapjustice.wordpress.com

Figure 95: Hanging execution of Moros during the Tagalog [Philippine] - American War.

~~ 69 ~~

Moors in America

Dr. Barry Fell (Harvard University) introduced in his 1983 book, *Saga America,* solid scientific evidence supporting the arrival of Muslims from North and West Africa centuries before Columbus. Dr. Fell discovered the existence of Muslim schools at several Nevada locations including Valley of Fire, Lagomarsino and Keyhole Canyons, Washoe and Hickson Summit Pass. Other sites were found in Allan Springs (Oregon), Mesa Verde (Colorado), Mimbres Valley (New Mexico) and Tipper Canoe (Indiana) dating back to 700-800 CE. Engraved on rocks in the arid western U.S, he found texts, diagrams and charts representing the last surviving fragments of what was once a system of schools - at both an elementary and higher levels. The language of instruction was North African Arabic written with old Kufic Arabic scripts. The subjects of instruction included writing, reading, arithmetic, religion, history, geography, mathematics, astronomy and sea navigation. The descendants of the Muslim visitors to North America are members of the present Iroquois, Algonquin, Anasazi, Hohokam and Olmec native people.

Figure 96: Excerpt from Fell's book, "Saga America."
Source: equinox-project.com

The Inyo Zodiac, in an area of petroglyphs discovered by J. H. Steward in 1929, east of Little Lake, Inyo County, California, but not hitherto recognized as a zodiac. The sun is shown to the right in the position it occupies at the time of commencement of the New Year in ancient America—the spring equinox. The constellations are shown in the order in which the sun passes through them, beginning on the right of the top row: Aries (March), Taurus (April), Gemini (May, the lower of two signs), Cancer (June, placed over Gemini), Leo (July), and Virgo (August); passing to the lower row, and reading now from left to right: Chelae, The Claws of the Scorpion, later separated as Libra (September), Scorpio (October), Sagittarius, shown as a bow (November), Capricornus (December), Aquarius, shown as a whale in ancient zodiacs, but here apparently damaged (February). *Epigraphic Museum replica, photo Peter J. Garfall.*

70
The Treaty of Peace and Friendship

between the Moroccan and Empire and the United States of America was the first treaty recognizing the United States as a Nation. It is the longest standing Treaty for the United States and among a very few the US has not violated or broken. It was put in place to ensure peace between the Moorish/ Moslems and Europeans/ Christians.

Treaty of Peace & Friendship
1787
Between Morocco and The United States

TO ALL PERSONS TO WHOM THESE PRESENTS SHALL COME OR BE MADE KNOWN- WHEREAS THE UNITED STATES OF AMERICA IN CONGRESS ASSEMBLED BY THEIR COMMISSION BEARING DATE THE TWELFTH DAY OF MAY ONE THOUSAND, SEVEN- HUNDRED AND EIGHTY-FOUR THOUGHT PROPER TO CONSTITUTE JOHN ADAMS, BEN- JAMIN FRANKLIN AND THOMAS JEFFERSON THEIR MINISTERS PLENIPOTENTIARY, GIVING TO THEM OR A MAJORITY OF THEM FULL POWERS TO CONFER, TREAT & NEGO- TIATE WITH THE AMBASSADOR, MINISTER OR COMMISSIONER OF HIS MAJESTY THE EMPEROR OF MOROCCO CONCERNING A TREATY OF AMITY AND COMMERCE, TO MAKE & RECEIVE PROPOSITIONS FOR SUCH TREATY AND TO CONCLUDE AND SIGN THE SAME, TRANSMITTING TO THE UNITED STATES IN CONGRESS ASSEMBLED FOR THEIR FINAL RATIFICATION.

Figure 97: Introduction of Treaty of Peace & Friendship.
Source: universalzulukemeticmuurs.net

71
The Moors Sundry Act of 1790

is an act passed by the South Carolina Legislature, acknowledging and respecting the status of Moors. Moors were subjects of the Moroccan Empire and were not (and are not) to be subjected to the laws governing blacks aka Negroes aka slaves.

Welcome!

The "Free Moors" of South Carolina

This published volume, which was originally for sale from the SCDAH, contains information dealing with the petition of the Moors. A report by the committee assigned to deal with their petition stated that they were not subject to the slave laws. There was no Act passed on this subject, however.

This manuscript was provided by the South Carolina Depart of Archives and History, Copyright ©1984, from their Research Library. This was available in book form from them, but is presently out of print. I personally thank the SCDAH for providing a copy of this record. All errors from my OCR software and proof reading are mine alone, and do not reflect on the outstanding quality of SCDAH work. FOC

The State Records of South Carolina

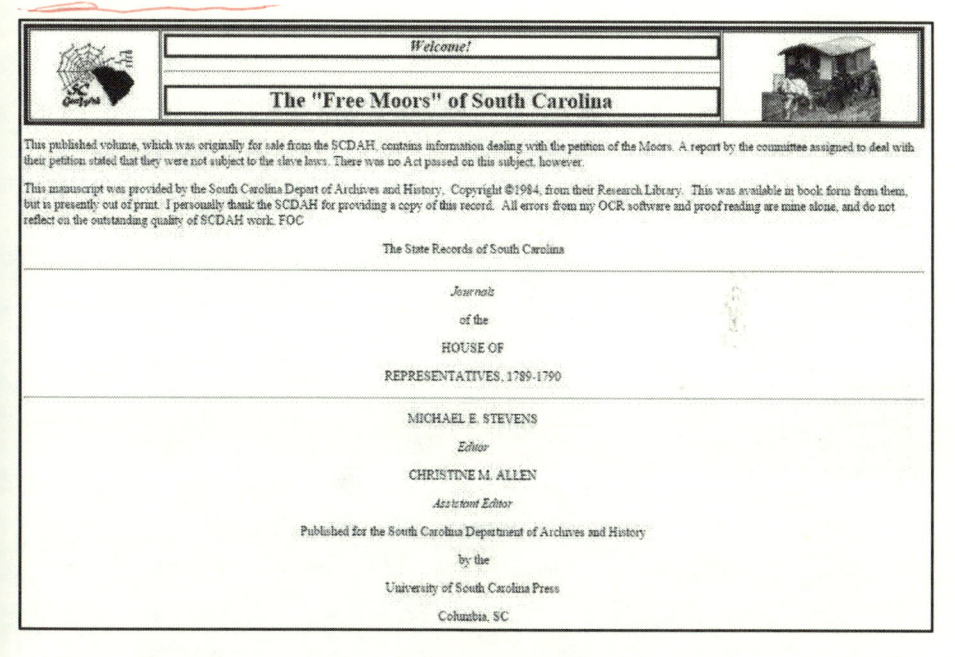

Journals

of the

HOUSE OF

REPRESENTATIVES, 1789-1790

MICHAEL E. STEVENS

Editor

CHRISTINE M. ALLEN

Assistant Editor

Published for the South Carolina Department of Archives and History

by the

University of South Carolina Press

Columbia, SC

Figure 98: Capture of Record of Petition from Free Moors of South Carolina. Source: State Records of South Carolina.
http://sciway3.net/clark/freemoors/journal.htm

72
Moorish Revival

or Neo-Moorish is one of the exotic revival architectural styles that were adopted by architects of Europe and the Americas in the wake of the Romanticist fascination with all things oriental. The Moorish-style castle known as the Pavilhão Mourisco is the centerpiece of the tour to the historical complex of Manguinhos, officially protected as part of Brazil's national heritage. This building, whose construction was based on a plan by Oswaldo Cruz himself, is one of Rio de Janeiro's finest pieces of architecture.

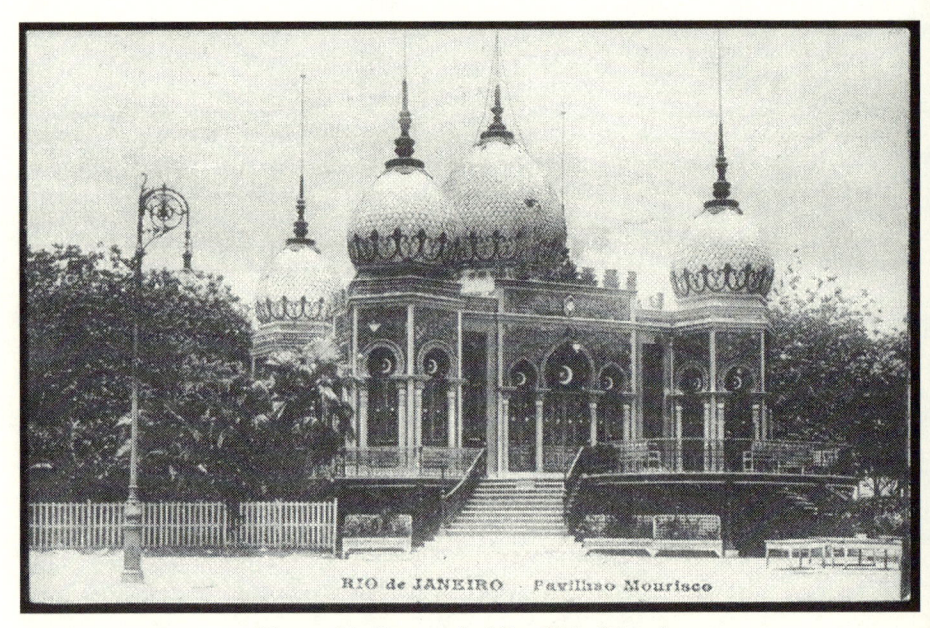

Figure 99: Postcard of Pavilhão Mourisco.
Source: produto.mercadolivre.com

73

The Moorish Science Temple of America, Subordinate Temple #5

aka The Canaanland Temple is the first Moorish Science Temple ever established in the North Amexem territory known as Canada. Peace to Grand Sheik Kudjo Adwo El and all of the Moors in Canaanland for their great works!!

Figure 100: Seal of the Moorish Science Temple Subordinate Temple #5 - Toronto.
Source Canaanland Moors.

74

Drew Ali's Visit with Marcus Garvey

This is a postcard from Prophet Noble Drew Ali to his wife after visiting the Honorable Marcus Mosiah Garvey while he was in an enslavement plantation, a.k.a. prison in Atlanta, Georgia. Note: One month after his visit from Noble Drew Ali, Marcus Garvey was deported by the U.S.

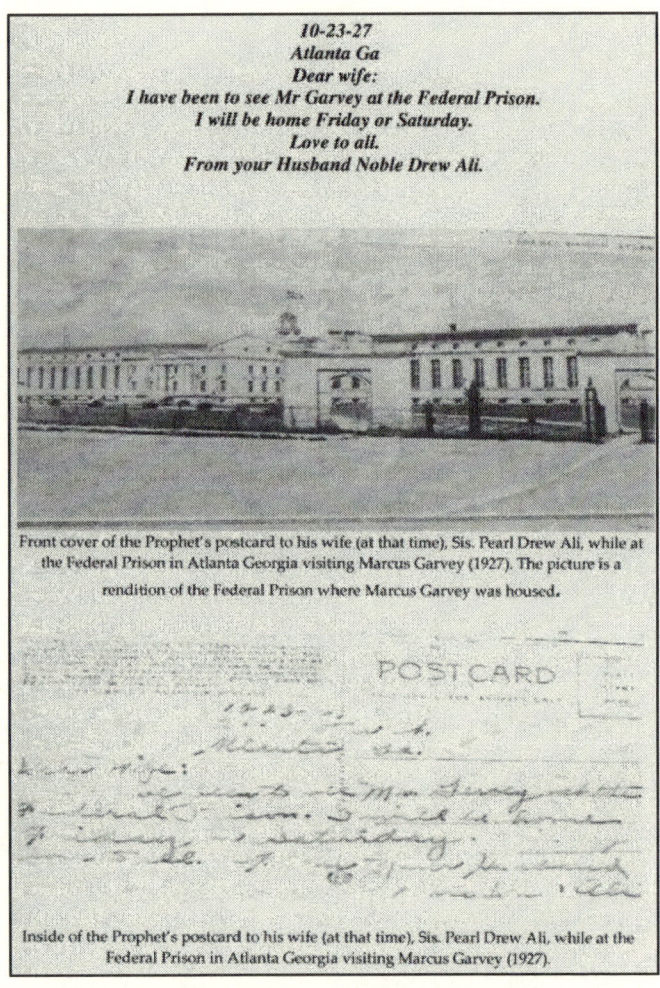

> 10-23-27
> Atlanta Ga
> Dear wife:
> I have been to see Mr Garvey at the Federal Prison.
> I will be home Friday or Saturday.
> Love to all.
> From your Husband Noble Drew Ali.

Front cover of the Prophet's postcard to his wife (at that time), Sis. Pearl Drew Ali, while at the Federal Prison in Atlanta Georgia visiting Marcus Garvey (1927). The picture is a rendition of the Federal Prison where Marcus Garvey was housed.

Inside of the Prophet's postcard to his wife (at that time), Sis. Pearl Drew Ali, while at the Federal Prison in Atlanta Georgia visiting Marcus Garvey (1927).

Figure 101: Postcard from Drew Ali to his wife, Pearl, relating his visit with Marcus Garvey.
Source: moorishoaklandstar.wordpress.com

75
F.B.J. Investigates the Moors

The FBI and the u.s. Government know very well who we, Moorish Americans are. So much so, that John Edgar Hoover ordered an extensive investigation into the Moorish Science Temple of America. You can view it today on the FBI's website.

http://vault.fbi.gov/Moorish%20Science%20Temple%20of%20America

The photos below are of Hoover wearing Moorish fezzes. Please note that they are marked, which is forbidden for Moorish Americans.

Figure 103: Hoover in fez 1.
Source: mindcontrolblackassassins.com

Figure 102: Hoover in fez 2.
Source yourworldnews.org

92

76

The One Federal Reserve Note

often referred to as the "one dollar bill" incorporates a variation of our Moorish Seal. In this portrayal, it's referenced as "The Great Seal". The difference being that our Moorish Seal has the eye of Horus connected to the pyramid's structure.

Please note that Federal Reserve notes are not true dollars. They function as I.O.Us.

Below are two examples to demonstrate the difference between a note and a dollar.

The certificate shown in Figure 104 is redeemable for one dollar in Silver. It is as good as having the silver coin or bar in your pocket. It's payable on demand.

Figure 104: 1957 Silver Certificate. Source usrarecurrency.com

The note in Figure 105, is not a certificate for one dollar in silver. It does not say it is payable on demand.

And it's not really from the United States of America.

The Federal Reserve Note is about as lawful as monopoly money.

Figure 105: Federal Reserve Debt Note. Source: freemasons-freemasonry.com

~~77~~
Audio Alchemy

The Reconquista eliminated Moorish rule. You will want to do your research on the Reconquista. The pictured artists are using Alchemy to blend our Moorish history and Science into our Hip Hop culture via music.

Figure 107: Sheik Ron Compilation CD. Source sheik-ron.bandcamp.com

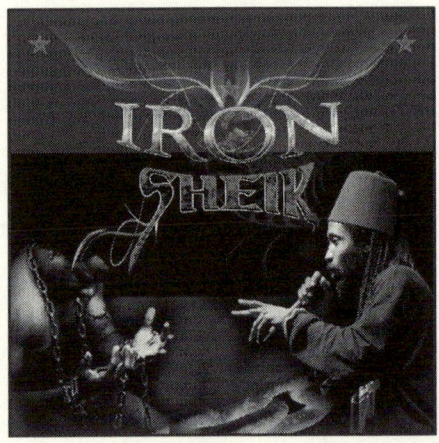

Figure 106 Iron Sheik 1. Source: lastfm.com

Figure 109: Pacific Standard Time by ClifSoulo. Source clifsoulo.bandcamp.com

Figure 108: Babylon Nightmare by Jahdan Blakkamoore. Source: israbox.net

IV. Need Proof?

Don't believe the information in this book. Perform your own due diligence. Investigate multiple sources. Find out the truth for your SELF. When you find out that it is true, don't keep it a secret. Let the world and BEYond know of our Moorish history.

This text could have matched every fact with a source so it would be easy for the readers to confirm its contents, but that would be a disservice. The mission of this book is not to walk your journey for you. Pick up these books and study. Go to the websites and study. Look up the Key Moorish Figures, listen to their lessons and...you guessed it! Study! It is insufficient to simply believe what one tells you, even if they are recognized scholars. A wise Moor once said "...are you a master mind and do not know that man knows naught by being told? Man may believe what others say, but thus he never knows...". You can believe us, or believe others, but if you do so, you will never know. You must seek the truth for yourself. Only then will you know.

Suggested Reading:

The Holy Koran of the Moorish Science Temple of America

Koran Questions for Moorish Americans

Othello's Children in the New World

The Story of the Moors in Spain

Golden Age of the Moors

The Lost Continent of Mu

World's Greatest Men of Color I and II

100 Amazing Facts about the Negro

Stolen Legacy

They Came Before Columbus

Sacred Drift

Spandau Mystery

Montauk Book of the Dead

Synchronicity and the Seventh Seal

Golden Trade of the Moors

Land of Osiris

Moses is Akhanaten

ALL of the books published by R.V. Bey Publications

ALL of the books published by Califa Media Publishing

Websites:

rvbeypublications.com

califamedia.com

moorishdirectory.com

moorishguidepost.org

iamhhtemple.org

hmoorishciviletter.net

moorishoaklandstar.wordpress.com

dralimelbey.com/moorish-holy-temple-of-science-of-the-world.html

northgatemoors.webs.com/

vault.fbi.gov/Moorish%20Science%20Temple%20of%20America

Motion Pictures:

True Romance

Black Knight

Celestine Prophecy

Robin Hood: Prince of Thieves

When the Moors Ruled in Europe

Key Moorish Figures

Taj Tarik Bey, Abdullah Talib Mosi Bey, Grand Sheik Nature El Bey, Sister Rasmariah Bey, Hakim Bey, Sabir Bey, Hannibal Bey, Rahme El Bey, Cozmo El, SetenRa Bey, Red and Blue Pill, Zahir Cassanova Nasir Bey, Krishna Ashira Bey, Jose Piementa Bey, Jabbar Gaines El, Selah Li Bey, C.M. Bey, El Hajj Malik El Shabazz, Mizraim Aleph El,

V. Outro

The citizens of all free national governments according to their national constitution are all of one family bearing one free national name. Those who fail to recognize the free national name of their constitutional government are classes as undesirables, and are subject to all inferior names and abuses and mistreatments that the citizens car to bestow upon them. And it is a sin for any group of people to violate the national constitutional laws of a free national government and cling to the names and the principles that delude to slavery.

I, the Prophet, was prepared by the Great God Allah to warn my people to repent from their sinful ways and go back to that state of mind to their forefathers' Divine and national principles that they will be law-abiders and receive their divine right as citizens, according to the free national constitution that was prepared for all free national beings. They are to claim their own free national name and religion.

There is but one issue for them to be recognized by this government and of the earth and it comes only through the connection of the Moorish Divine National Movement, which is incorporated in this government and recognized by all other nations of the world. And through it they and their children can receive their Divine rights, unmolested by other citizens that they can cast a free national ballot at the polls under the free national constitution of the States Government and not under a granted privilege as has been the existing condition for many generations.

You who doubt whether I, the Prophet, and my principles are right for the redemption of my people, go to those that know law, in the City Hall and among the officials in your government and ask them under an intelligent tone, and they will be glad to render you a favorable reply, for they are glad to see me bring you out of darkness into light. Money doesn't make the man, it is free national standards and power that makes a man and a nation. The wealth of all national governments, gold and silver and commerce belong to the citizens alone and without your national citizenship by name and principles, you have no true wealth, and I am hereby calling on all true citizens that stand for a National Free Government, and the enforcement of the constitution to help me in my great missionary work because I need all support from all true American citizens of the United States of America. Help me to save my people who have fallen from the constitutional laws of government. I am depending on your support to get them back to the constitutional fold again that they will learn to love instead of hate, and will live according to Love, Truth, Peace, Freedom, and Justice, supporting our free national constitution of the United States of America.

I Love my people and I desire their unity and mine back to their own National and Divine standard because day by day they have been violating the national and constitutional laws of their government by claiming names and principles that are unconstitutional. If Italians, Greeks, English, Chinese, Japanese, Turks, and Arabians are forced to proclaim their free national name and religion before the constitutional government of the United States of America, it is no more than right that the law should be enforced upon all other American citizens alike. In all other governments when a man is born and raised there and asked for his national descent name and if he fails to give it, he is misused, imprisoned, or exiled. Any group of people that fail to answer up to the constitutional standards of law by name and principles, because to be a citizen of any government you must claim your national descent name. Because they place their trust upon issue and names formed by their forefathers.

The word Negro deludes in the Latin language to the word nigger; the same as the word "colored" deludes to anything that is painted, varnished and dyed. And every nation must bear a national descent name of their forefathers, because honoring thy fathers and they mothers, your days will be lengthened upon this earth. These names have never been recognized by any true American citizen of this day. Through your free national name you are known and recognized by all nations of the earth that are recognized by said national government in which they live. The 14th and 15th Amendments brought the North and South in unit, placing the Southerners who were at that time without power, with the constitutional body of power. And at that time, 1865, the free national constitutional law that was enforced since 1774 declared all men equal and free, and if all men are declared by the free national constitution to be free and equal since that constitution has never been changed, there is no need for the application of the 14th and 15th Amendments for the salvation of our people and citizens.

So, there isn't but one supreme issue for my people to use to redeem that which was lost, and that is through the above statements. Then the lion and the lamb can lie down together in yonder hills. And neither will be harmed, because Love, Truth, peace, Freedom and Justice will be reigning in this land. In those days the United States will be one of the greatest civilized and prosperous governments of the world, but if the above principles are not carried out by the citizens and my people in this government, the worst is yet to come, because the Great God of the Universe is not pleased with the works that are being performed in North America by my people and this great sin must be removed from the land to save it from enormous earthquakes, diseases, etc. And, I, the Prophet, do hereby believe that this administration of the government being more wisely prepared by more genius citizens that believe in their free national constitution and laws and through the help of such classes of citizens, I, the Prophet, truly believe that my people will find the true and Divine way of their forefathers, and learn to stop serving carnal customs and merely ideas of man, that have never done them any good, but have always harmed them.

So, I, the Prophet, am hereby calling aloud with a Divine plea to all true American citizens to help me to remove this great sin which has been committed and is being practiced by my people in the United States of America, because they know it is not the true and Divine way and, without understanding they have fallen from the true light into utter darkness of sin, and there is not a nation on earth today that will recognize them socially, religiously, politically or economically, etc. In their present condition of their endeavorment in which they themselves try to force upon a civilized world,

101

they will not refrain from their sinful ways of action and their deeds have brought Jim-Crowism, segregation, and everything that brings harm to human beings on earth. And they fought the Southerner for all these great misuses, but I have traveled in the South and have examined conditions there, and it is the works of my people continuously practicing the things which bring dishonor, disgrace, and disrespect to any nation that lives the life. And I am hereby calling on all true American citizens for moral support and finance to help me in my great missionary work to bring my people out of darkness into marvelous light.

—From The Prophet Noble Drew Ali

Post Script

About the back panel:

15. All men see not the Triune Allah. One sees Him as Allah of might; another as Allah of thought; another as Allah of love. Chapter 10, H.K.M.S.T.A.

The first collaborative work of three primary contributors to the shelves of Califa Media Publishing.

Grand Sheik Brother Kudjo Adwo El is renowned for his enthusiasm in putting the sword to dirty Moors and admonishing the rest to be active not passive.

Grand Sheik Brother Rami Salaam El in his broadcast lectures calls attention to those issues that might otherwise escape the notice of studious Moors focused on loftier thoughts.

Sheikess Tauheedah S. Najee-Ullah El was recognized and appointed a trustee of this Divine and National Movement due to her continued sacrifice and efforts on behalf of our beloved Prophet and Nation.

The High Priestess Card of the Ancient Science of Tarot depicts the columns Boaz, Jachin and Solomon's Temple. Study teaches us Boaz represents Severity, Jachin represents Mercy, and both flank and protect the entrance to the secret/ source of life; The Temple.

Works Cited

Black, H.C. *Black's Law Dictionary*. 4th. St.Paul, MN: West Publishing, 1957.

City of Palestine. *Welcome to Palestine, Illinois. The Pioneer City*. 2010. http://www.pioneercity.com/history.html (accessed March 1, 2015).

G.S. Salaam El, Rami. *Moorish Jewels Emerld Edition*. Redondo Beach, CA: Califa Media Publishing, 2014.

GS. Adwo El, Kudjo. *Nationality, The Order of the Day*. Redondo Beach, CA: Califa Media Publishing, 2014.

Jackson El, Kevin. *For the New Moors: A Draw*. Riverdale, IL: Califa Media Publishing, 2015.

Jerusalem Virtual Tours. *Moroccan Gate or Bab Al-Magharebah*. 2009. http://www.holiestcity.com/VTengInfoTMag.html (accessed March 1, 2015).

Jewell, Elizabeth and Frank Abate, eds. "New Oxford American Dictionary." Oxford, England: Oxford University Press, 1998.

Moon, Peter. *Synchronicity & the Seventh Seal*. New York: Sky Book, 2004.

Morro Bay.com. *History Of Morro Rock And The Nine Sisters*. 1995. http://www.morrobay.com/rock.htm (accessed March 1, 2015).

Noble Drew Ali, Prophet. "101 Koran Questions for Moorish Americans." In *"I'm Going to Repeat Myself.": A Collection of Artifacts Authored by the Prophet Noble Drew Ali & the M.S.T. of A.*, by Tauheedah S. Najee-Ullah El, 14-22. Redondo Beach, CA: Califa Media Publishing, 2014.

—. *The Holy Koran of the Moorish Science Temple of America Circle 7*. Chicago: Moorish Guide Publishing, 1928.

Oaktown Art. *Oaktown Art.com*. 2010. http://oaktownart.com/2010/03/05/fox-theater/ (accessed March 2, 2015).

Rogers, J.A. *100 Amazing Facts About the Negro with Complete Proof: A Short Cut to the World History of the Negro*. St. Petersburg, FL: Helga M. Rogers, Publisher, 1980.

Roman Empire.Net. *Marcus Opellius Macrinus*. n.d. http://www.roman-empire.net/decline/macrinus.html (accessed March 2, 2015).

Scott v. Sandford. 60 U.S. 393 (1857) (The Supreme Court, 1857).

Skhs. Najee-Ullah El, Tauheedah. *Moors in America: A Compilation*. Redondo Beach, CA: Califa Media Publishing, 2014.

Spider879. *Moors in European Coat of Arms*. Feb. 13, 2013. http://www.abovetopsecret.com/forum/thread927046/pg1 (accessed March 11, 2015).

The Holy Bible. n.d.

Webster, Noah. *Webster's American Dictionary of the English Language*. New Haven, CT: B.L. Hamlen, 1828.

Table of Figures

FIGURE 1: J.A. ROGERS I
FIGURE 2: LEGAL DEFINITION OF MOOR 5
FIGURE 3: PROPHET NOBLE DREW ALI, FOUNDER OF THE MOORISH SCIENCE TEMPLE OF AMERICA, 1925 9
FIGURE 4: PROPHET NOBLE DREW ALI SURROUNDED BY VARIOUS DIGNITARIES. 1928 10
FIGURE 5: PHOTO FROM FIRST NATIONAL CONVENTION OF THE 10
FIGURE 6: PROPHET NOBLE DREW ALI, 1925 11
FIGURE 7: PROPHET NOBLE DREW ALI, FOUNDER OF MODERN ISLAM IN AMERICA 11
FIGURE 8: NOBLE DREW ALI SENDING THE UNIVERSAL SIGN OF DISTRESS ON BEHALF OF THE MOORISH NATION IN AMERICA 11
FIGURE 9: SIS. PEARL DREW ALI 12
FIGURE 10: DEPICTION OF RUTH THE MOABITESS. 13
FIGURE 11: COVER FOR CORMEGA'S ALBUM "INDUSTRY." 14
FIGURE 12: ST. VICTOR THE MOOR. 15
FIGURE 13: MARKER FOR ST. BENEDICT THE MOOR CATHOLIC CHURCH – 16
FIGURE 14: ST. BENEDICT THE MOOR. 16
FIGURE 15: MARCUS OPELLIUS MACRINUS 17
FIGURE 16: "SIGH OF THE MOOR" BY MARCELINO DE UNCETA. 18
FIGURE 17: CALIFIA, QUEEN OF CALIFORNIA 19
FIGURE 18: DUCHESS SOPHIA CHARLOTTE OF MECKLENBURG-STRELITZ. 20
FIGURE 19: HIS MAJESTY KING KALUKAUA 21
FIGURE 20: ESTAVANICO ("ESTEBAN THE MOOR"). SOURCE: TRIPDOWNMEMORYLANE.BLOGSPOT.COM 22
FIGURE 21 PAGE FROM MORIAEN 23
FIGURE 22: COAT OF ARMS FOR WAREGEM, WEST FLANDERS, BELGIUM. 24
FIGURE 23: DEPICTION OF THE BATTLE OF BADR. 25
FIGURE 24: ZENATA BEREBERS OF NORTH AFRICA 26
FIGURE 25: COVER OF CHARLES SUMNER'S "WHITE SLAVERY IN THE BARBARY STATES." 27
FIGURE 26: CHARLES SUMNER 1811-1874 27
(FIGURE 27: PHOTO OF MORO SULTAN OF TALICK AND DATUS (CHIEFTAIN) CIRCA 1904. 28
FIGURE 28: PHOTO OF MORO YOUTH. CIRCA 1904. 28
FIGURE 29: MINDANAO, SECOND LARGEST AND SOUTHERNMOST ISLAND OF THE PHILIPPINES. 29

FIGURE 30: CEYLON MOORS ON STEPS OF GRAND MOSQUE, NEW MOOR STREET, COLOMBO, SRI LANKA. 1901 30
FIGURE 31: PORTAIT OF GANNIBAL BY EUGENE DELACROIX 31
FIGURE 32: MEMORIAL OF GANNIBAL. SOURCE: STEPHENHICKS.ORG 31
FIGURE 33: DUSE MOHAMMED ALI. SOURCE: "NATIONALITY, THE ORDER OF THE DAY" BY G.S. KUDJO ADWO EL 32
FIGURE 34: HON. MARCUS GARVEY. SOURCE: "NATIONALITY, THE ORDER OF THE DAY" BY G.S. KUDJO ADWO EL 32
FIGURE 35: "ABOUT C.M. BEY." 33
FIGURE 36: EL HAJJ MALIK EL SHABAZZ AT THE GREAT PYRAMIDS 34
FIGURE 37: FOUNDERS OF HIPHOP BEING HONORED IN FRONT OF NEW YORK CITY HALL. AFRIKA BAMBAATAA BEY CENTER, IN BEADS. SOURCE: NYDAILYNEWS.COM 35
FIGURE 38: IMAGE OF STEVIE WONDER FROM THE EARLY 1970S WEARING SHIRT WITH ZODIAC GLYPHS. SOURCE: DISCOGS.COM 36
FIGURE 39: ALBUM COVER FOR THE SOUNDTRACK TO THE FILM BAMBOOZLED. SOURCE: DISCOGS.COM. 36
FIGURE 40: BACK PANEL OF YASIIN BEY'S "THE ECSTATIC" ALBUM 37
FIGURE 41: MUSICAL LEGENDS DAMIAN MARLEY, AND NAS PERFORMING THEIR AMAZING COLLABORATIVE ALBUM, DISTANT RELATIVES. 38
FIGURE 42: 1927 SKETCH OF MU BY COL. J. CHURCHWARD. 40
FIGURE 43: SATELLITE IMAGE OF RAPA NUI. 41
FIGURE 44: MAP OF RAPA NUI SHOWING STATUE SITES 41
FIGURE 45: PERSPECTIVE RENDERING FOR MOAI TUTURI (L) AND MOAI AHU TONGARIKI (R) 42
FIGURE 46: STAND OF "MOAI" 42
FIGURE 47: BODY OF MOAI STATUE 43
FIGURE 48: MAURYAN EMPIRE UNDER ASHOKA 44
FIGURE 49: TEMPLE MOUNT, JERUSALEM 45
FIGURE 50: DOME OF THE ROCK, TEMPLE MOUNT, JERUSALEM 45
FIGURE 51: POLITICAL MAP OF NORTH AFRICA, MAURITANIA CIRCLED. 46
FIGURE 52: THE LOGOS 7/ BROKEN SEVENTH SEAL 47
FIGURE 53: HOLY KABBAH (CIRCLED) IN MECCA, ARABIA. SOURCE: GOOGLE.COM 47
FIGURE 54: AL ANDALUS AT ITS HEIGHT OF POWER ON THE IBERIAN PENNINSULA. SOURCE: MUSEUMOFTHECITY.ORG 48
FIGURE 55: MOSLEM AND CHRISTIAN PLAYING MUSIC. SOURCE: MUSEUMOFTHECITY.ORG 48
FIGURE 56: PATIO DEL CANALE 49
FIGURE 57: THE LADIES POND. SOURCE: IMARABE.ORG 49

FIGURE 58: CLOSE-UP OF THE FOUNTAIN OF LIONS. 50
FIGURE 59: PATIO DE LOS LEONES, NASRID PALACE, ALHAMBRA. 50
FIGURE 60: MOORISH EMPIRE IN THE WEST 51
FIGURE 61: PHOTO OF THE PYRAMID OF THE MOON TAKEN FROM THE PYRAMID OF THE SUN. 52
FIGURE 62: FACADE OF NEW YORK CITY CENTER, MANHATTAN, NY. 53
FIGURE 63: CENTRAL SYNAGOGUE, MANHATTAN, NY. 54
FIGURE 64: IMAGE OF NOBLE DREW ALI PLAZA. 55
FIGURE 65: PLACARD FOR MOOR'S CHARITY SCHOOL, COLUMBIA, CT. 56
FIGURE 66: MARKER FOR CITY OF PALESTINE, ILLINOIS. 57
FIGURE 67: MOAB, UTAH CITY MARKER. 58
FIGURE 68: FOX OAKLAND THEATER. TELEGRAPH AVENUE FACADE WITH MARQUEE 59
FIGURE 69: PYLONS OF FOX OAKLAND THEATER 59
FIGURE 70: WINDOWS OF FOX OAKLAND THEATER 60
FIGURE 71: FRONT VIEW OF FOX OAKLAND THEATER 60
FIGURE 72: MAP OF MAURITANIA AVENUE, OAKLAND CALIFORNIA. IMAGE SOURCED FROM GOOGLE MAPS 61
FIGURE 73: MORRO ROCK. 62
FIGURE 74: THE CANAANITE TEMPLE. 63
FIGURE 75: COVER OF "STOLEN LEGACY" ORIGINALLY PUBLISHED 1954. 65
FIGURE 76: LOS MOROS. 67
FIGURE 77: EARLIEST KNOWN DEPICTION OF A GAME OF CHESS. 68
FIGURE 78: EXCEPT FROM JOURNAL PAPER ON IBN AL-AWAM, GEOGRAPHICAL REVIEW JAN. 1943. 69
FIGURE 79: "THE CONNOISSEURS." 70
FIGURE 80: DEPICTION OF SCENE FROM "THE SONG OF ROLAND." 71
FIGURE 81: SAMPLE OF MOORISH USE OF MATH IN INTERIOR DESIGN. 72
FIGURE 82: SAMPLE OF THE USE OF FRACTALS IN MOORISH DESIGN. 73
FIGURE 83: UNIVERSITY OF TAMPA'S PLANT HALL. 74
FIGURE 84: STATUE OF MOORISH KNIGHT IN CHAINMAIL ARMOR. 75
FIGURE 85: MOORISH BROCHE BY CARTIER. SOURCE ES.PAPERBLOG.COM 75
FIGURE 86: CODOGNATO BROCHE OF MOOR- ENGRAVED GOLD, SILVER & GEM STONES. 75
FIGURE 87: COAT OF ARMS FROM LOKA CASTLE SKOFJA LOKA MUSEUM. 76
FIGURE 88: CHANDRAGUPTA MAURYA, FOUNDER OF THE MAURYA EMPIRE. 77
FIGURE 89: EXPANSION OF MOORS INTO THE IBERIAN PENINSULA. 78
FIGURE 90: COLUMBUS ON HIS ARRIVAL ON HISPANIOLA. 80
FIGURE 91: FROM THE COLLECTION OF SIR. THOMAS WRIORTHESLEY / COVER OF ANCIENT AND MODERN BROITONS BY D. MAC RITCHIE. 81

Figure 92: Serving of moros y christianos. 82
Figure 93: Image from Bud Dajo Massacre, 1906. 83
Figure 94: Moro warriors circa 1900. 84
Figure 95: Hanging execution of Moros during the Tagalog [Philippine] - American War.
.... 85
Figure 96: Excerpt from Fell's book, "Saga America." 86
Figure 97: Introduction of Treaty of Peace & Friendship. 87
Figure 98: Capture of Record of Petition from Free Moors of South Carolina. 88
Figure 99: Postcard of Pavilhão Mourisco. 89
Figure 100: Seal of the Moorish Science Temple Subordinate Temple #5 - Toronto. 90
Figure 101: Postcard from Drew Ali to his wife, Pearl, relating his visit with Marcus
    Garvey. 91
Figure 102: Hoover in fez 2. Source yourworldnews.org.. 92
Figure 103: Hoover in fez 1. 92
Figure 104: 1957 Silver Certificate. 94
Figure 105: Federal Reserve Debt Note. 94
Figure 106 Iron Sheik 1. 95
Figure 107: Sheik Ron Compilation CD. Source sheik-ron.bandcamp.com 95
Figure 108: Babylon Nightmare by Jahdan Blakkamoore. 95
Figure 109: Pacific Standard Time by ClifSoulo. 95

Other Titles from Califa Media®

Moorish Children's Guide to History and Culture

Moorish Jewels: Emerald Edition

Moors in America

Moslem Girls' Training Guide a.k.a. The Sisters' Auxiliary Handbook

Nationality, the Order of the Day

Noble Drew Ali Plenipotentiaries

Official Proclamation of Real Moorish American Nationality

Well, Come to Klanada

You Are NOT Negro, Black, Coloured, Morisco nor an African Slave

Who Stole the Fez, Moors or Shriners?

Califa Uhuru Series

Vol. 1: Holy Koran of the Moorish Holy Temple of Science, Circle 7

Vol. 2: "I'm Going to Repeat Myself.": A Collection of Artifacts Authored by Noble Prophet Drew Ali and the M.S.T. of A.

Vol. 3: Mysteries of the Silent Brotherhood of the East a.ka. The Red Book, a.k.a. Sincerity

Vol. 4: Califa Uhuru; A Collection of Literature from the Moorish Science Temple of America

Made in the USA
Monee, IL
15 February 2020